JEA   US

Trumpeting by Nature
An Efficient Guide to Optimal Trumpet Performance

Outskirts Press, Inc.
Denver, Colorado

The opinions expressed in this manuscript are solely the opinions of the author and do not represent the opinions or thoughts of the publisher.

Trumpeting by Nature
An Efficient Guide to Optimal Trumpet Performance
All Rights Reserved
Copyright © 2007 Jeanne G. Pocius
V1.0

This book may not be reproduced, transmitted, or stored in whole or in part by any means, including graphic, electronic, or mechanical without the express written consent of the publisher except in the case of brief quotations embodied in critical articles and reviews.

Outskirts Press
http://www.outskirtspress.com

ISBN-10: 1-4327-0261-0
ISBN-13: 978-1-4327-0261-8

Library of Congress Control Number: 2006940665

Outskirts Press and the "OP" logo are trademarks belonging to
Outskirts Press, Inc.

Printed in the United States of America

TABLE of CONTENTS

Dedication		v
Acknowledgements		vii
Witness		viiii
Introduction		ix
Chapter 1	The Roadmap: *How to Use This Book*	1
Chapter 2	How <u>DO</u> You Hold the Trumpet?	3
Chapter 3	Sitting Pretty: *Posture for the Trumpet Player*	15
Chapter 4	K.I.S.S. with Your Lips *& Anchor Spot*™	24
Chapter 5	Well, Shut My Mouth!--*NOT!*	48
Chapter 6	Power of the Pout: *Developing the Lower Lip*	64
Chapter 7	What's Your Angle? *Your Natural Pivot & Angle*	78
Chapter 8	To Buzz or Not to Buzz? *That's the Question*	86
Chapter 9	T^4: *Terrific Tongue Technique Tips*	94
Chapter 10	Hold That Tiger! *Harnessing Air Power*	111
Chapter 11	Daily Diagnostic CHOPCHECK™	121
Chapter 12	Swim Through the Woodshed: *Efficient Practice*	152
Chapter 13	Extreme Techniques: *Save It Til You Need It!*	161
Chapter 14	Fix-Its: *Recovering from Injury or Fatigue*	166
Chapter 15	Making Lasting Changes	190
Chapter 16	Painting A Personal Style: *The Palette Approach*	197
Chapter 17	Walking the Walk: *Practicing What You Teach*	205
Chapter 18	Equipment: *How Many Mouthpieces in Your Barrel?*	231
Chapter 19	Navigating the Jungle:*Avoiding Professional Pitfalls*	250
Chapter 20	"Give It Back! It's Mine!" *Trumpet Philosophy*	267
Chapter 21	Teacher Tributes: *The Trumpet Family Tree*	272
Chapter 22	In Conclusion: *The Journey Continues*	283
Appendix I	Biography of Jeanne Gabriel Pocius	285
Appendix II	Excerpts from TPIN Postings	289
Appendix III	Daily Diagnostic CHOPCHECK™	334
Appendix IV	Equipment Sources & Services	340
Bibliography	Recommended Books	344

DEDICATION

I have been blessed throughout my life with excellent teachers, colleagues, friends, family members, and students.

It would be impossible to name every person who has had an influence on my growth as a musician and a teacher, and to single out one person in particular from those ranks would be to slight others of equal importance to me.

However, God has blessed me with one person who has opened my eyes, my ears, my heart, and my spirit as no one else.

This book would not be in your hands were it not for the love, support and inspiration of my beloved soul mate, Terry Casey.

So with great admiration, appreciation, and love, this work is dedicated to you, Terry, so that the world will know about your contribution to the trumpet community.

I love you, now and always!
Jeanne

ACKNOWLEDGEMENTS

First, I'd like to thank Chris Kline and Lori Ewen, my advisor-representatives at Outskirts Press.

I'd also like to thank Stanton Kramer, and Marty Rooney for their help with the images in the book, and Nick Mondello, my publicity agent.

It goes without saying that I owe an immense debt to all of my teachers through the years, both in music and other subjects, who have been tremendous sources of enlightenment and inspiration to me:

Catherine Wade, Marty Goldstein, Frances Sullivan, Peg Thompson, Lilli McDouglas, Peter Morse, Elizabeth Camacho de Navarro, John Adamo, Eleanor Mullaney, Barbara Pollard, Frank Reilly, Shirley Baldwin, Algis Balinskas, Tim Quinn, Bill Vacchiano, Mel Broiles, Bruce Bellingham, Avo Somer, Dick Strawser, David Maker, Mary Collier-Jones, Father Joe Kugler, Sister Eucharista, Dan Patrylak, Jerry Callet, Dr. Charles Colin, Jeff Holmes, Charles Treger, Walter Chesnut, Ed Winiker, Bo Winiker, Victoria Avedisyan, Rolf Smedvig, Father Oshagan Minassian, and, of course, all the many hundreds of students and colleagues past and present who have constantly challenged and inspired me!

I must also pay tribute to my beloved grandmother, Isabel Constance Perkins, who has always been, and continues to be my hero in every sense of the word!

Finally, the most important tribute of all:

WITNESS

I am a follower of Jesus Christ of Nazareth.
I believe that He is the Messiah,
the embodiment of God's love for us
and that He redeemed us
through His death upon the cross.

All that I am and all that I do, particularly in playing and teaching the trumpet, I offer up in prayer and thanksgiving to the Living God.

I humbly pray that God will bless your heart and soul and all those who hear the sound of your trumpet.

God bless, and Take Care!
Jeanne Gabriel Pocius

INTRODUCTION

In my many years as a trumpet teacher and "chop doc," I have encountered countless numbers of trumpeters who struggled in playing the trumpet.

None of us is born with a trumpet mouthpiece in our tiny fist, but each of us has the capacity to learn to play the trumpet efficiently, that is "with the greatest amount of return for the least amount of effort."

For many years, my students have asked me to put my ideas about making music on the trumpet into written form. I have deferred until now, believing that there are sufficient trumpet method books already in print to cover any etudes necessary to the development of good trumpet technique.

However, I have come to realize that, though many books exist to develop "high range," "power," "flexibility," ability to transpose, and facility in tonguing; there are not many books dealing with the facility of music making on the trumpet. (Homage, of course, to the great Mel Broiles' book "The Art of Trumpet Playing"!)

Of course, the most important gift I can give you is the certain knowledge that you are your own best teacher! Take the time to get to know your body, your chops, your equipment, and your tastes, because the greatest teacher/coach in the world still cannot climb inside your body or your head to adjust things.

At best, a good teacher provides his or her student with a kind of roadmap to the journey of becoming a great musical artist: the individual must still do the driving themselves!

The following pages are presented in the hopes that trumpeters may find some inspiration to undertake that journey, with the greatest amount of personal comfort and ease.

"How do you **DO** that?" "You make it look so easy!" "Makes trumpet playing look as easy as blowing your nose!" "Loudest trumpet player I have ever heard!" "Softest trumpet player I have ever heard!" "I didn't know a trumpet could sound like that!"

Comments such as the preceding are typical reactions from trumpet players who are experiencing their first exposure to efficient trumpet playing.

And yet, it is not impossibly difficult to make music with a trumpet.

An efficient approach to trumpet playing entails learning to work **with** the body's natural tendencies, rather than against them.

Too often, band directors and trumpet teachers are concerned with mere cosmetics: "hold your bell up" "mouthpiece half and half" "center your mouthpiece" "grip your trumpet firmly in your left hand" "trumpet parallel to the floor" etc.

In reality, few trumpeters play with an exactly centered embouchure that enables the trumpet to be held straight-out, parallel to the floor. Why not?

This is because a trumpeter would have to have an exactly concentric shape to his/her face, with perfectly straight and flat front teeth and perfectly aligned jaws in order to play this way. (I haven't met anyone like that in close to fifty years of music making, have you?)

In my opinion, "gripping the trumpet firmly in the left hand" leads to pathology in the embouchure, because tension travels from the hand, up the arm, into the neck and the embouchure itself.

At this point, most trumpeters are at a loss: "How <the h*** am I supposed to play, then?!!???" My answer: "efficiently!"

In the words of Daniel Patrylak, founder of the Eastman Brass Quintet, we must learn to use "relaxed tension." While that might seem like an oxymoron, it really isn't! Perhaps a clearer phrasing of it might be "relaxed flexion," because when we are flexing muscles pertinent to the task at hand without isometrically or isotonically flexing unnecessary muscles we are able to be more relaxed and efficient in our approach to music making on the trumpet.

In the following pages, you will learn a variety of approaches and techniques designed to assist you in becoming a more efficient trumpet player. I am not, however, **dictating** to you that you "must" play this way! I tell my students repeatedly: "Listen to everything. Apply what works for you. Discard the rest."

I do ask that you send me your thoughts and comments on what I have written. The process of becoming an efficient teacher is like that of becoming an efficient trumpeter: ongoing. It is impossible to be general enough for every conceivable reader. Therefore, if you feel I could have stated something in a different way that might have made it easier to understand or more appropriate to **your** learning style, please contact me through TPIN (Trumpeter Players' International Network, an email list maintained by Dr. Michael Anderson. **www.tpin.org**) or via email, directly: jgpocius@yahoo.com .

Be aware that even the most thorough teacher can only be a partial guide to you in your journey to becoming a trumpet artist. We can and do give you a road map to follow: approaches and techniques that may make the journey easier for you. But you must drive the road by yourself! (We cannot even be "co-pilots" except in your memory and imagination!)

It's worth the trip!!!

Have a safe, happy, successful journey!

God-speed and Take Care!

CHAPTER 1

The Roadmap:
How to Use This Book

This really isn't a book meant to be read like a novel, from cover to cover, in page order! You are certainly welcome to read it that way, but you don't need to do so.

Instead, I'd suggest that you peruse the table of contents and see which topics jump out at you. You should visit these chapters first, since they are probably areas in which you could use a little encouragement or challenge to your present ideas.

You might find that the appendices interest you first (exercises, bibliography, biography, equipment sources and services, and supplementary material, including a listing of helpful books and resources). Or you may find that the chapters on embouchure or breathing interest you first.

Please <u>don't</u> try to read the entire book in one sitting, or your head will be swimming! Take frequent breaks and do other things during those breaks (much like you should when practicing!).

No matter which order you choose to pursue in reading the book, I hope you will keep an open mind, and take frequent rests! Sometimes you may find that something that is difficult to grasp at first reading will become clearer after a break. Don't feel that every technique or idea applies to you (some will, some won't).

I tell my students repeatedly: "Listen to everything. Apply what works for you. Discard the rest."

The journey begins here. Enjoy the ride!

CHAPTER 2

How **DO** You Hold the Trumpet?

Many trumpet players grew up believing that it is necessary to hold the valve casing of the trumpet in a death-grip. Some even believe that the right pinky finger serves as an octave key (consciously or not: I wonder if their first teachers were woodwind players who couldn't get over the idea that an octave key was necessary to change octaves!).

Of those players, some never learn to use their first and third valve slides to adjust intonation (and if they DO adjust intonation, they will distort their embouchure to do so, thus losing the quality of sound of a natural embouchure). Some of those who **do** learn to use their slides wind up with carpal tunnel syndrome, or a twisting technique of the mouthpiece against the embouchure, or some other distortion of posture, hold, or embouchure.

I, too, originally was taught to "grip the trumpet firmly in your fist around the valve cluster."

Much later in life I learned how much easier it is to play with relaxed hands, and when I discovered the *Shulman System* (see Appendix IV, on equipment), I learned that a combination of good posture and balancing the trumpet not only made it easier to play, but also improved the sound!

Shulman System

Most of you don't have a *ShulmanSystem* yet. My hope is that manufacturers will eventually offer it as a standard option with the purchase of a trumpet. Of course, that will probably begin with high-end professional instruments, then go down the price chain, but I hope that even beginning instruments will eventually offer the *ShulmanSystem* as matter-of-factly as the manufacturers of saxophones offer neck-straps.

Until that point, however, let's consider a few possible ways to break yourself of the "death-grip" hold on your trumpet. After all, if I put my hands around your neck and began to squeeze, <**HARD!**> you wouldn't feel much like singing, would you? Then why do you expect your trumpet to "sing" when you're choking it to death?!!???

Okay, then let's begin with the

LEFT HAND

1. Examine your left hand:

    - Are your fingers curled tightly around the valve casing?
    - Is your pinky finger separated from the ring finger by the third valve slide?
    - Do your knuckles turn white as you ascend or crescendo?

2. First, let's try simply balancing the horn on the palm of your left hand.

    - You should be able to play a comfortable second line G this way, preferably even a slur from that G to the third space C.
    - If you cannot produce these notes, at least try to play a stable low C.

It might be harder than you thought it would be, but that's okay because you've only just begun this trip into more efficient trumpet playing. Don't be too hard on yourself: remember, you are your own best teacher, and as a teacher you wouldn't try to discourage a student who was just starting out, would you? Of course not!

I want you to learn a typical technique I use with my students: $\boxed{T^3}$

That is: Always **TRY THREE TIMES**!!!
There is a strong psychological reason for this, as well as a cognitive reality:

Sometimes you learn best by taking a break! Attempting a new skill three times in succession gives you ample time to see if "you've got it!" without leading you to become frustrated and causing you to develop bad habits to compensate by distorting the proper action. Also, taking a break allows your subconscious mind to continue to work on the problem.

Ever work on a math problem before going to sleep and find that you've discovered the solution when you awaken? Same process.

So now is a good time to take a break and listen to some good music for trumpet as played by Maurice Andre, Philip Smith, Nick Payton, etc. After all, you need to stretch your legs periodically on a long trip, don't you?

All rested? Good. Let's get back to work.

First, again, we're going to BALANCE the trumpet on the left hand, but this time we're going to do so on the first two fingers of the left hand. That's right, the index finger and middle finger of the left hand should balance the trumpet, under the bell, just past the third valve slide. The left thumb should be on the opposite side of the valve cluster/casings, about opposite the crack between those first two fingers on the other side of the valves.

Here are some pictures to help you:

As you can see, the left ring finger is resting in the third valve slide ring (but NOT curled back toward you), and the pinky rests on the outside of the third slide (helping to balance the horn).

 Also, there is space between your left palm and the left side of the valve casings. If you hold your trumpet bell up, you should be able to look between your palm and the valve casings.

Sometimes it can be helpful to place half of a solid rubber ball between your palm and your valves.

If you have a *Shulman System* this is all fairly simple, if not, it may take some adjustment on your part. Be sure to keep the fingers of your left hand straight, not curved, or you might be tempted to strangle your trumpet again.

What you're going to learn to do is to throw the third slide out with the back of the left middle finger, and to pull the third slide back in by pulling with the left ring finger. It's not as hard as it sounds, but you must make sure that your third slide is well lubricated and well "broken-in" so that it moves smoothly and without hesitation.

You can obtain "o" rings to put on the slide to keep it from clicking and to make it easier to release when you are extending it.

> **N.B.:** You may need to modify this technique slightly if you have triggers installed on your first and third slides, but it is still possible to stay relaxed while using triggers, too!

You will need to practice throwing the slides out (do this without putting the trumpet up to your face at first, so any awkwardness on your part doesn't lead to your lips getting smashed by the mouthpiece!).

Remember to keep your first and third valves down when you are throwing the pertinent slides out so you don't get vapor lock (that loud, clicking noise you get when valves are not compressed and you throw the slides can lead to a loss of compression in the valves over time).

Next we'll discuss the

RIGHT HAND

The right hand is really simple because all it does is push the valves down and get out of the way for them to come back up, right?

Oops. I forgot that most of us have been told to "bang the valves down forcefully" or maybe "curve the fingers into a hook/claw before pressing the valves down, HARD!"

Hmm. No wonder so many trumpet players quit sometime in junior or senior high! It HURTS to distort the hand position! (And can cause serious problems like carpal tunnel syndrome, over-use syndrome, etc).

For the record: **<u>DO NOT "BANG" your valves</u>**!!!

That's right; I just said, "Do not bang your valves."

Why not?

Because they won't come up any faster if you bang them, and you're likely not only to hurt yourself, but you may be "banging the valves down" at an angle which will lead to uneven wear in the valves/casings, compression loss, etc.

So what do you do instead?
Think of moving your fingers, quickly, but under water.

What happens to the motion? It becomes smoother, doesn't it? That's what you're going to do with your valves now.

In order to do that, I've found that most players (unless you have very large hands) benefit from placing the tip of the thumb under the lead-pipe and between the first and second valve slide. You don't have to "ram" that tip in there, just place it gently. This becomes the anchor for your right hand.

Again, this is even easier when you're using the *ShulmanSystem*, but once you realize that **THE RIGHT HAND DOESN'T HOLD THE TRUMPET** it makes it much easier to manipulate the valves.

Keep your right pinky finger on TOP of the pinky ring (unless you are using a mute with your left hand, or turning pages).

Letting your fingers remain slightly curved (but more on the straight side), place the pad of your fingers on top of the valve buttons.

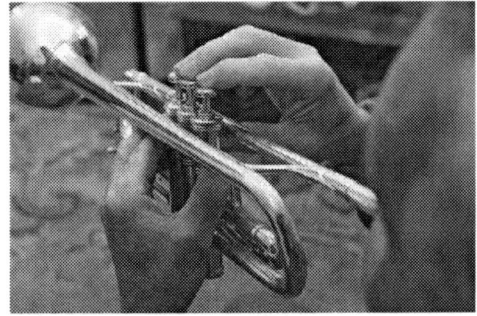

Remember that the right thumb is placed slightly between and below the first two fingers, (I'm told by younger students that this reminds them of the hand position for throwing a "curve ball" if that helps you to remember this position). Your right hand should look like a side-ways capital "U."

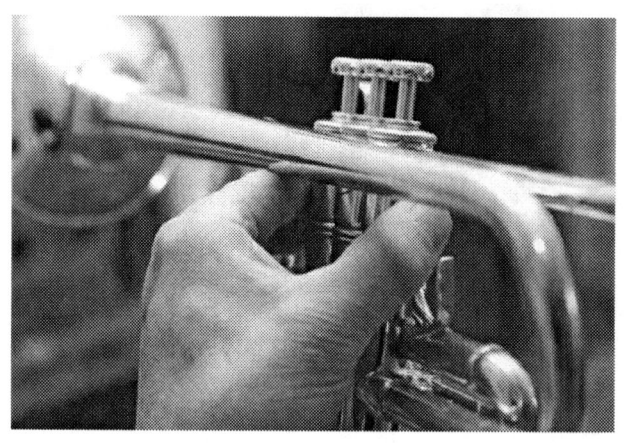
At all times, remember that the hands should be only carefully **BALANCING** the horn, not "gripping" it. If there is tension in your hands, there will be tension in your arms, your torso, your neck and ultimately, in your chops.

Now, before we go on to more new ideas, I'd suggest that you practice with these new hand positions for a week or two. You may find that it takes some time for you to adopt them and that you slip backward a bit, but that's okay!
It's a bit like missing your exit and having to double back on a road trip: it really doesn't matter when you're not on a strict time frame, does it? Of course not! In the long run you'll be a better player, able to do more, and more easily.

If you're like most trumpeters, you'll find yourself turning more and more to these hand positions because they really DO make it easier to play.

A final word concerns adaptive techniques.

My very first student was a very small boy, with tiny hands, whose doctor had recommended he take up the trumpet to help him cope with asthma.

Because a cornet was not an option, I devised a sort of adaptive device out of a wire music stand to help him support the bell of the trumpet.

On another occasion, I was able to assist a disabled colleague by creating a device to hold the trumpet by making a cradle out of wood and Velcro and using a cymbal boom stand to enable him to roll his wheelchair up to the trumpet so he could maintain his chops while dealing with temporary paralysis.

A former teacher of mine, Robert Lemons, made use of a bent shank on his mouthpiece to assist him with his jaw formation and avoid a severe downward pivot. Bob Reeves makes a Chuck Findley model mouthpiece for which the original was bent at 12 degrees. He can make the angle whatever you need it to be. (See Appendix IV for more information)

I share these ideas with you to encourage you to be creative in adapting devices to assist our lesser-abled fellow trumpeters.

Remember: where there is a will, there is a way. If we, as teachers and colleagues, encourage others to strive in spite of challenges we become stronger and better persons, and by extension, better musical artists.

Time for another pit-stop. See you soon!

CHAPTER 3

SITTING PRETTY:

Posture for the Trumpet Player

Is there a "proper way" to sit or stand when playing the trumpet? Can the way you sit or stand affect the sound coming out of your bell, the range you can hit or techniques you can perform?

Perhaps you remember a band teacher telling you "Sit up! Trumpets, Bells UP!" or something similar. No doubt your mother admonished you "Don't slouch!" or "Stand up straight!"

But have you ever really considered *why* it is important for a trumpet player to think about good posture?

Here are some factors to consider:

Whether you are standing or sitting to play, it is crucial that you maintain a slight arch in your lower back. This allows the lower back muscles to support the airstream as it is expelled.

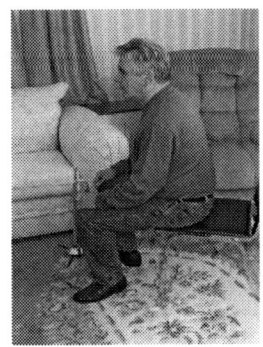

You may find it helpful, if standing, to either stand on tip-toe, or to sit on the forward edge of a stool to assist you in maintaining the proper lower back arch.

Try these exercises:

I. Sit with your back away from the back of the chair.

II. Bend forward from the hips until your chest meets your upper legs (or as far as possible toward that position).

III. Now sit upward, allow your abdomen to slightly protrude, your lower back to arch inward (toward your waist), and your shoulders and upper back to sit parallel to your hips. It may help to think of "sitting your shoulder blades downward toward your waistline."

IV. Sit in relaxed fashion, without slouching. Now imagine that there is a string that extends downward through the center of your skull, through your spinal cord, between your buttocks and into the floor. Imagine that the cord is pulling you slightly upward toward the ceiling without introducing tension into your body.

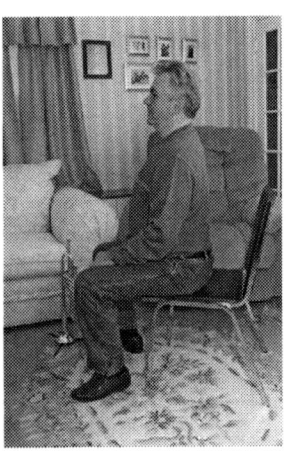

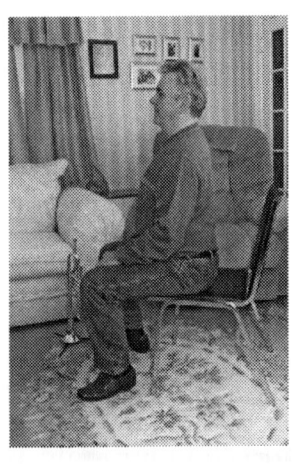 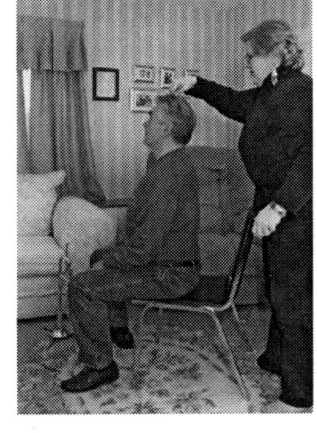

Good Posture, Head Down   String Pulling You Upward

It is also very important to keep your head in alignment with your spine. This dissipates any tension in the trapezius and sterno-cleido-mastoid muscles (the area between the shoulder blades, leading up into the neck, and the muscle that runs from your ribcage up into your neck and jaw).

Try these exercises:

A. While sitting up straight in a chair, or standing without slouching, keep your shoulders down and back and relaxed.

Now thrust your head forward, without allowing your shoulders to roll forward.

Notice the tension between your shoulders, in your shoulders and in your neck. You may also notice that there is tension in your neck and jaw. This can translate into tension in your embouchure as well. Obviously, this particular etude (exercise) is designed to help you recognize something you should avoid when playing!

B. A good way to dissipate (get rid of) the tension you just introduced into your neck and shoulders is the following:

Keep your shoulders down and back.

Roll your head gently toward one shoulder, and then the other (be careful to avoid any sort of strain, and if you have ANY pain or osteoarthritis in your neck, please check with your doctor before doing this or any other neck exercise!).

Finally, move your head in a gentle circle, from front to back, going first clockwise, then counterclockwise.

C.   Check that you are not hyper-extending your neck by leaning your head too far backward:

Bend your head back as far as possible, then gradually return it to an upright position in which the neck is as relaxed as possible. You may find that by slightly "bobbing" your head (like one of those bobbing animals in the back window of a car), you are able to locate the position that gives you the greatest degree of relaxation.

Keeping your chest expanded and your shoulders down and relaxed helps you to refill your air supply more efficiently, and helps to maintain relaxation throughout the torso.

Try these exercises:

A.   Fill your lungs completely, by breathing inward, forming your mouth into a round "O" as if you were saying the word "HOME" (but do not make any sounds with your voice!)

Now sigh the air out, emptying your lungs completely, but do not allow your chest to collapse.

When your air is all gone, allow the vacuum in your chest to expand the lungs naturally and fully. Your abdomen/belly should collapse inward but your upper chest should stay expanded. You should find that it is very easy to re-inspire or re-inflate your lungs this way without producing any excess tension.

B.   Now repeat the process you just did above; but this time, allow your chest to collapse as the air empties.

You'll find that it takes much more effort to re-inflate your lungs once the chest has collapsed.

You may also find that it causes more tension in your torso to breathe in after you have allowed the chest to collapse.

Ideally, there should be no tension between the base of the sternum and the lips themselves.

Support of the air column is given primarily by the upper abdominal and lower back muscles, with some additional support by the intercostals (between the ribs) and the muscles of the chest wall.

There are numerous approaches that I have found to be helpful in establishing and maintaining good posture. The first of these is doing a daily physical routine of sit-ups or crunches.

N.B.: *<u>Always</u> check with your physician before beginning any regular physical activity!*

Glen Adsit, the Director of Bands at the Hartt College of Music at the University of Hartford, introduced me to basic Tai Chi. This is an Eastern technique of physical meditation that incorporates steady, deep, measured breathing with prescribed poses and motions.

I have found Tai Chi to be helpful not only for myself and my trumpet students, but also for special needs students in my band programs because it encourages relaxation, awareness, and good breathing. I cannot recommend it more highly. Please see the appendices for more information about Tai Chi.

Another technique that I have incorporated into my playing and teaching is the Alexander Technique, which makes use of proper body alignment and kinesthetics (movements). This is particularly helpful in preventing repetitive stress injuries, sciatica, and sore or tired backs.

Barnes and Noble publishes a good introductory book on the system, and there are seminars around the United States at which you can learn more, as well as individual practitioners with whom you can consult.

The Longy School, in Cambridge, MA, offers programs in both Alexander and Dalcroze Eurhythmics systems. I encourage you to contact them directly (please see appendices).

Another advantage to good posture is that it can help to prevent injury, including hernias and injury to the sciatic nerve.

The *sciatic nerve*, when inflamed or injured, can cause pain that shoots from the back or thigh down into the leg, foot and toes.

A *hernia* is the protrusion of an organ or part of an organ through a membrane or cavity wall, usually the abdominal (tummy) cavity. A diaphragmatic, or hiatal hernia is the protrusion (bulging) of the lower esophagus, stomach or intestine into the thoracic(chest) cavity through the hole in the diaphragm that allows passage of the esophagus.

When a hernia occurs, it is important to seek medical attention as soon as possible to avoid complications. Surgery to repair hernias now makes use of a mesh-like material that tends to make such repairs more long lasting, but will require an extended period for recovery that may entail time away from practice and performance.

Proper posture and kinesthetics (movement) can help to prevent such injuries from occurring and extend your playing life.

In summary, whether standing or sitting to play, try to keep your head and spine in alignment, your abdomen relaxed or flexed inward (depending upon register and dynamic volume) and your chest expanded.

CHAPTER 4

K.I.S.S.* With Your Lips

*Keep It Soft & Supple

Do you remember being told when you were young that playing the trumpet would give you "tough lips"? Or maybe you looked at photos (or even actual older players) with deep grooves or even thick scar tissue on their lips and thought "Gee! Am I going to look like that?"

Not necessarily so, at least not if you learn to practice the "K.I.S.S." technique and *Keep It Soft and Supple* when you play.

How do you do that? It's simple, really.

The basic impetus to sound creation on the trumpet is vibration of the lips. The lips need to vibrate against each other, thus setting the standing column of air within the trumpet into vibration. The speed of the vibration and the strength of the vibration determine the pitch and dynamic level produced.

Many trumpet players forget this basic premise, though.

They'll beat on their chops, night-after-night: blowing too hard, pressing too hard, with tight corners and a flaccid (flabby) center of the lips that causes them to BANG between the hard surface of the teeth and the hard surface of the mouthpiece.

Eventually tiny pressure blisters (that stinging sensation inside the lips really DOES do damage, you know!) turn into calloused tissue, cornification (hardening) occurs on the surface of the lips, the lips stop vibrating freely and you have to blow much harder and use much more pressure to get ANY sound at all!

Excess free-buzzing or mouthpiece buzzing without follow-up pedal tone practice can also work to stiffen and toughen the lips.

It doesn't have to be that way. You can learn to play with soft, flexible chops that will give you extended range of pitch and dynamics, easy response, endurance and finesse.

Here's how to start the process:

KISS A FISH

Well, not really! But you DO want to purse your lips slightly forward, in front of your teeth, as if you were trying to kiss a fish, but repulsed by the idea.

What this does for you is it allows the soft, wet inner surfaces of the lips to touch. (You can't purse your lips without doing this.)

You can then learn to roll the red (inner membrane) of your lips outward or inward, depending upon the type of tone color you wish to produce. This also creates a sort of cushion into which you can comfortably set the mouthpiece to create a good seal between your two lips and between the lips and mouthpiece.

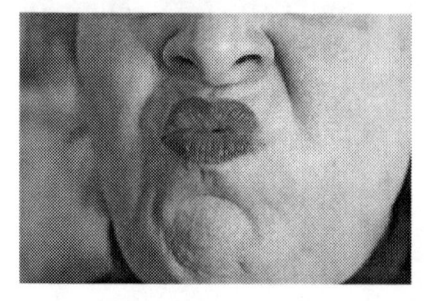

Outward Roll 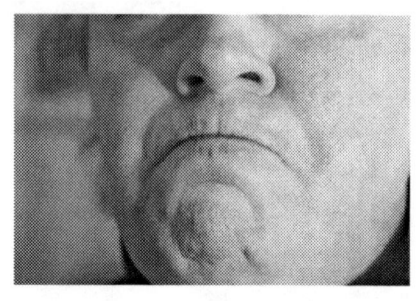   Inward Roll

If this is difficult for you, at least try to roll out the lower lip (gently!) so that you can set the upper lip gently into the soft, wet inner surface of the lower lip. Again, this is subtle, though you may need to exaggerate at first until you gain control over your lips.

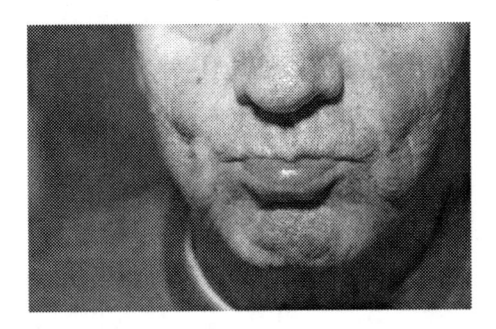

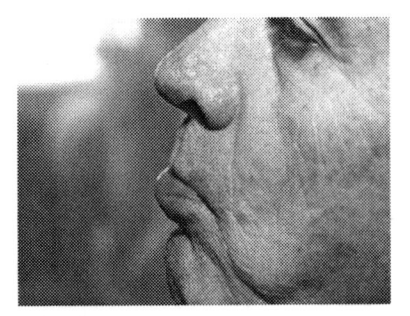

This is a necessary prerequisite to your identifying your natural Anchor Spot™. Some players refer to this as their "sweet spot" or "set point."

It doesn't matter so much WHAT you call it as long as you find it and use it!

There are several reasons for this:

1. Your Anchor Spot™ is the point at which your lips have the best compression.

2. Using your natural Anchor Spot™ will enable optimal use of your natural angle and pivot.

3. Knowing where your Anchor Spot™ is located will enable you to play quickly and accurately much sooner than if you employ a "hit or miss" approach. (I've known trumpeters who would take hours trying to find their "sweet spot" and then had no chops left with which to play!)

4. Making use of your Anchor Spot™ will help you to choose the best possible mouthpiece for your natural chops.

Now this doesn't mean that it is not possible to play upon a setting other than your natural Anchor Spot™, but trying to play in a way that is contrary to your natural, anatomical setup is not going to help you achieve your maximum potential.

And your natural setup is as individual as YOU are: no two trumpeters are the same and no two trumpeters have exactly the same setup.

For a trumpet teacher to insist that everyone play in the same central spot, with the horn in the same angle or pivot (perpendicular/straight out), in the same position vis-à-vis up and down (half and half or 2/3's 1/3 or vice versa) is, in my humble but experienced opinion, highly irresponsible.

It is possible to play while distorting the natural set and function of the lips, but results may be inconsistent at best. Is your sound full and pure in all registers? Are you placing the upper, inner rim of the mouthpiece above the vermilion margin (the spot where the red lip membrane meets the white muscle of the upper lip)?

This is crucial to avoid injury to the delicate lip membrane, particularly with someone who has not played before, or who has not played in some time.

Please note: there are some players, with very thick, very fleshy lips, who manage to play low on the upper lip, but it always results in scarring (which impedes lip vibration, and ultimately finesse of playing).

Many of my students with thick, fleshy lips have found great success with learning to roll the upper lip inward (causing the red to "disappear") which allows them to make use of the orbicularis oris muscle to control the fine motor embouchure muscles when playing.

Here is the process you'll need to follow to

IDENTIFY YOUR Anchor Spot™

Because your lips' anatomy is uniquely yours, we need to take into account a number of factors in setting up your embouchure.

1. Most important of all is finding your best compression point (the spot at which your lips seal best, which is where the center of your embouchure should be located--and ultimately where the basic tone is produced). This is found by using the following procedure: (watch yourself in a mirror)

    WITHOUT tightening your corners, press your lips as strongly as possible against each other, in front of your teeth, then **pop** the lips apart.

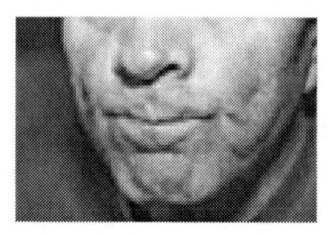

Compressing Lips 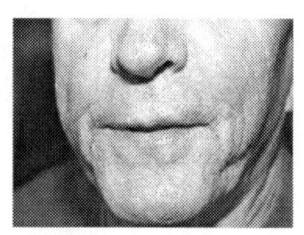   Releasing Compression

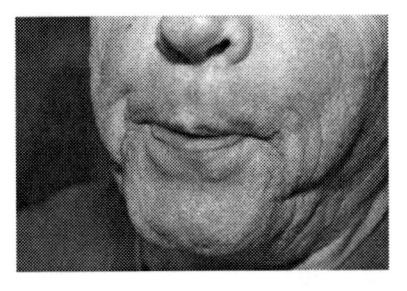

You should notice a brief, white spot on the lower lip (it will fade quickly, so watch carefully!).

Repeat the process a couple of times to be sure you've seen it.

Now, place the tip of your pinky finger into the flesh of your UPPER lip, right above where you saw the white spot on your lower lip, but in the white of the upper lip, just above where the white meets the red.

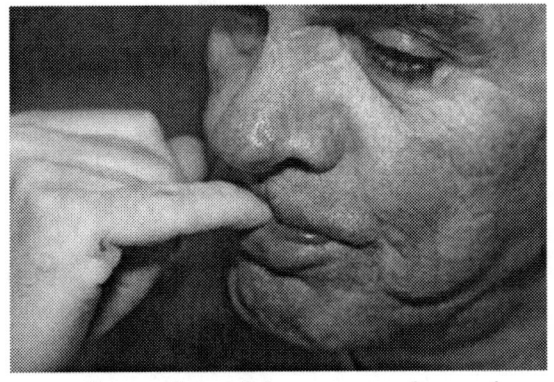

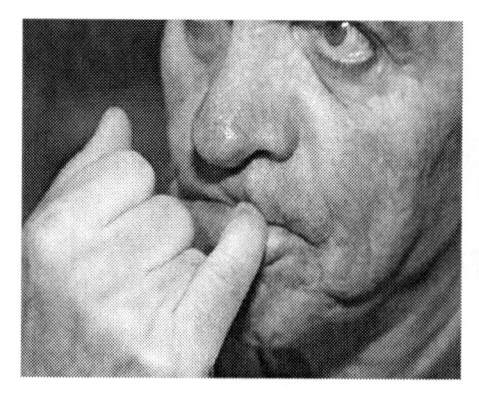

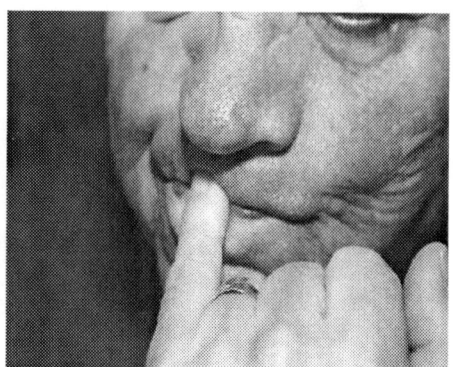

Press in slightly, and push side-to-side and up-and-down. You should find that the muscle gives way slightly in this area (which is usually roughly triangular in shape).

This is the area in which the orbicularis oris muscle joins back to itself and attaches to the maxilla bone and also has is related to the size and shape of the philtrum, but for your purposes it shows you where you'll set the inner, upper rim of the mouthpiece.

Now, you'll note that I advocate setting the mouthpiece into the flesh of the upper lip. Some players spend time talking about which lip is "active" or vibrating while playing. It doesn't really matter whether you are an upstream or downstream player, the mouthpiece must *anchor* in the upper lip.

Let me explain why:

If you examine the structure (anatomy) of the orbicularis oris muscle, you'll note that above the band of muscle which surrounds the upper lip(and has a twin below the lower lip) there is an inverted *V* just above the philtrum, and just below the *ala*, (which is the convex, flared portion of the nose, where it joins the upper lip),within which is non-muscular tissue.

This is, I believe, the optimal point at which to place the center of the upper, inner rim of the mouthpiece (and is the area which my *Anchor Spot ID* post describes as being the area which "gives way" when manipulated after identifying the strongest point of compression between the two lips).

It is this inverted *V* that leads me to recommend placement or anchor of the mpc here, along with the factors that:

1. The upper lip is attached to the maxilla, which is a stationary bone.

2. The lower lip is attached to the mandible, which is a moving bone.

3. The upper lip's musculature is more limited, as it is affected chiefly by the orbicularis oris, its other muscular relationships tend to create the opposite effect to good chops (vis-à-vis *smile chops*), with the zygomaticus (which draws the upper lip up and out when flexed), the levator labii superioris (which raises the upper lip when flexed), and the risorius (which aids compression, but also tends to draw the lips outward).

4. The musculature of the lower lip is more extensive, thus allowing that lip to move more freely (and necessitating that lip's being free-to-move, hence my concerns about locking it down by anchoring the mpc on the lower lip). Of course, the orbicularis oris (the sphincter muscle which enables the *drawstring bag* effect of closing or pursing the lips) affects the lower lip AND the upper lip. And the risorius affects the lower lip in a similar manner to the upper lip.

The difference between the lips occurs with the following muscles:

The Muscles which affect the Mandible (lower jaw), to which the lower lip is attached, include the following:

<u>Lateral Pterygoid</u>: enables the protruding (pushing forward) of the mandible (lower jaw), also enables side-to-side movement of same..

<u>Medial Pterygoid</u>: elevates and protrudes mandible, also enables side-to-side movement of same.

<u>Temporalis</u>: elevates and protrudes (pushes out) mandible.

<u>Depressor labii inferioris</u>: lowers lower lip (drops it, opening oral cavity, freeing compression, allowing freer buzz)

<u>Platysma</u>*: depresses(drops) mandible, draws outer part of lower lip downward and back (pouting)

<u>Mentalis</u>*: elevates AND protrudes lower lip, as well as pulling tissue of chin upward (pouting)

You'll note that I've starred the final two muscles on this list, because I feel that their freedom from being hampered is SO important to efficient (easy) trumpet sound & flexibility.

The bottom line is that we need to use the chops as efficiently as possible, in order to use them with an appropriate airstream to produce the greatest ease and power in trumpet playing.

I strongly believe that anchoring the mpc on the lower lip is detrimental in the long run to optimal playing. Please note that *anchoring the mpc* is the process of setting the mpc slightly **INTO** the slightly flexed muscular tissue of the upper lip.

This is not to say that this *anchoring* is not, in itself also flexible, and should *breathe* (move) slightly inward or outward based on multiple playing factors, including speed (velocity) and quantity (volume) of air flowing through the closed lips. Nor is it to suggest that it is not possible, indeed preferable for many, if not most, players to make use of some manner of *pivot* (movement up/down) and/or angle (movement left/right to maintain good seal) in playing.

It is my opinion that it is far better to hold the horn lightly, allowing the HORN to move while playing, than it is to hold the horn rigidly and force the face/lips/jaw to contort to change registers/dynamics/style etc.

The best approach is that which focuses on efficiency in all things:

- Adequate air (but not too much, nor too little)
- Least amount of movement necessary to achieve the desired effect in playing (be that register change, timbre change or whatever)
- Most relaxed hand positions (Best is merely balancing the horn for most playing, except at the absolutely loudest dynamics---any type of strong *grip* of the horn, with EITHER hand, will lead to tension which will impede the optimal technical abilities of the player)
- Most aligned and relaxed body posture possible (to enable optimal muscular support of the airstream and reduce any unnecessary tension in the body)
- Shortest possible stroke of the tongue that will achieve the desired sound production (sometimes that may result in mere interruption of the airstream, other times it may require impeding the flow of air for the strongest attack).

Dan Patrylak advocates a process, which he describes as **Relaxed Tension**.In other words, make use of the flexion of necessary muscles, but otherwise cultivate the greatest ease and relaxation.

The product is that of a style of trumpet playing which APPEARS to be virtually effortless. And trust me, it's far more impressive to audiences to make the most difficult music appear effortless than it is to share with them the efforts involved in producing the end product of BEAUTIFUL MUSIC.

ANCHORING THE MOUTHPIECE IN THE UPPER LIP

1. You'll want to place the center of the mouthpiece rim here at the Anchor Spot™, but make sure that you catch the INNER, upper rim just above the vermilion margin (the **shelf** where the white and red meet).

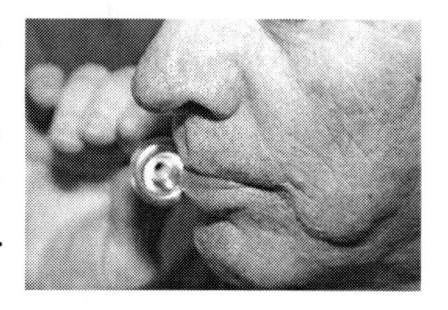

For some folks it's a bit higher, but it must be AT LEAST above that meeting point of muscle and membrane.

Often, if the upper lip is relatively short from nose to edge, it can be helpful to tip the mouthpiece upwards and use the width of the mouthpiece rim to guide you in rolling the mouthpiece down to the proper spot.

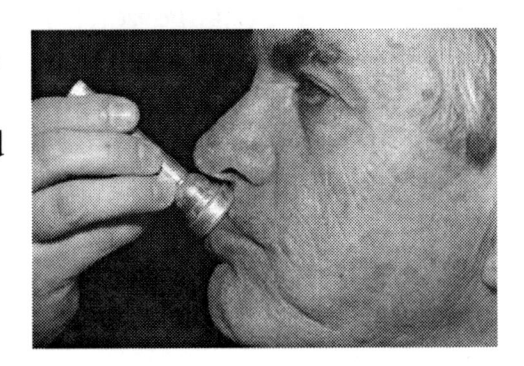

2. Now wet and close your lips, and roll the mouthpiece downward just enough to affect a seal between the mouthpiece and the closed lips. You may need to angle slightly left or right to accommodate your tooth structure, and/or slightly downward or upward to accommodate your jaw structure to affect the seal. Make the pertinent adjustments as you play.

3. The key is to stay very relaxed as you play. Use lots of air, in the middle register. You should begin by playing a second line G or third space C.

4. The biggest change you'll likely notice is that notes will speak more readily when you play on your proper anchor spot. You'll also note that lip flexibility (lip slurring) is more reliable. In addition, your sound will be more centered and balanced.

5. It is also VERY important that you keep your back molars separated/ jaws open, even though you are keeping your lips closed. This puts the greatest work in embouchure onto your lower lip, which has better capacity for doing that work by virtue of its being free to move, unlike the upper lip, which is tied to the maxilla bone. You may find your lower lip growing very tired.

   Allow yourself ample opportunity to rest.

6. You may find it helpful to keep the tip of your tongue forward, over the top edge of the bottom teeth, to assist the lower lip and keep it from collapsing inward. Do NOT, however, allow the tongue to thrust between the lower and upper lips because that would disturb the seal between them, which is so important for optimal tone quality.

7. Finally keep your hands relaxed. Do not **Grip** the trumpet: merely balance the trumpet on your left hand, and keep the right pinky OUT of the ring (it's NOT an **octave key!**) Allow the trumpet to **breathe** (move slightly) as you play. Remember to allow the lips' motion, though more subtle, to **flow** just as the air must!

KEEP THE CENTER SOFT

Keeping the center of your lips soft will make it much easier to get the lips to speak at all dynamic levels. It will allow you to crescendo or decrescendo without your sound breaking up. It will enable you to make good use of breath attacks as well as tongue attacks, and help you to control the releases (ends) of notes better.

Finally, a soft center to your lips will allow you to play without excess compression of the lips against each other. Because the lips are soft in the center, and slightly pursed in all registers, it will take only a very tiny "pinch" of lip against lip to make a change from one partial (harmonic) to another.

The short term advantage of this is a greatly increased ability to do lip slurs, even across large intervals. The long term advantage is a huge increase in endurance since your lips don't have to work as hard as they did before you learned to do this technique.

Of course, optimal use of pivot (up to down movement of the horn) and angle (left to right movement of the horn) and understanding the proper use of air and air support will contribute to the success of this technique, too!

See Chapter 7 for more information on angle and pivot, and Chapter 10 for more information on optimal use of your air and air support.

One of the best ways to help develop soft, vibrating lips is to practice the following:

PLAY ELEPHANT FARTS

Well, not exactly, but this is the metaphor I use to help young students remember the sound of double-low pedal tones.

These are pedal tones, which begin two octaves (or more) below low C below the treble staff. They are played with an adaptive embouchure technique and are an ETUDE, not to be confused with the normal playing embouchure at all.

Because I prefer to dispel tension from my playing, I do not recommend playing pedal tones between low F# (1/2/3 fingering) below the staff and the first pedal C (one octave below the C below the treble staff). Although very experienced players can make use of these notes without causing problems with their playing (and can move from pedals through the regular registers with ease), most trumpeters make use of excess tension in their lips, jaw, and throat to achieve these unnatural pedals.

The double-low pedals, on the other hand, do not induce tension when performed properly. They DO soften the lip membrane, preparing it to vibrate and produce tone. They loosen and limber the embouchure muscles, free the airstream, and help to increase blood flow to the lips and muscles, which make up the embouchure.

Here's the process to follow to produce the double-low pedals (elephant farts):

1. Roll bottom lip outward into a gentle pout. (Be careful to avoid rolling out too far: keep your corners relaxed!)

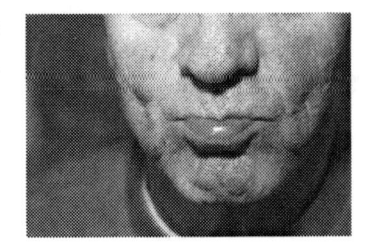

2. Set your top lip gently down, into the soft, wet inner surface that was exposed when you rolled out the bottom lip.

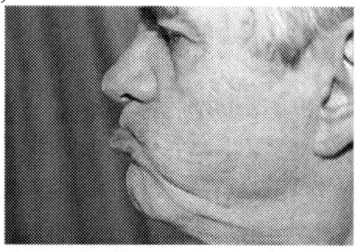

3. Tip your trumpet bell upwards and rest the top rim of the mouthpiece gently HIGH on the upper lip.

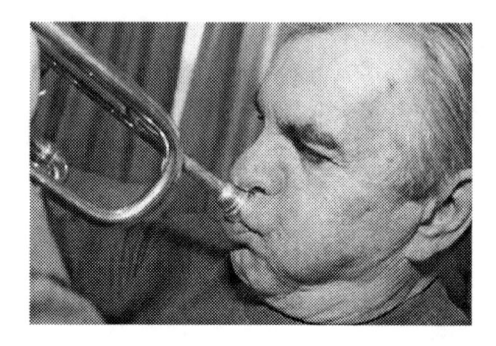

4. Without pressing down or in with the mouthpiece rim, slide it down to your Anchor Spot™.

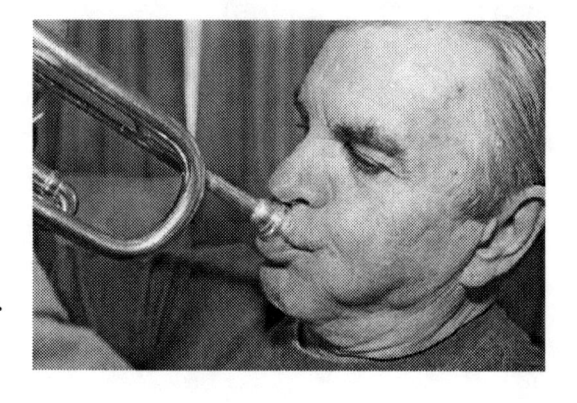

5. Tilt the mouthpiece <u>slightly</u> down until the complete mouthpiece rim is in contact with both lips (the lower lip may sit outside the lower rim of the mouthpiece: don't be concerned about this if it happens, as long as both lips are in contact with each other and with the mouthpiece!) Don't allow the mouthpiece to separate the lips, though.

6. Take a deep breath (through your nose) and blow <u>very</u> gently to achieve a very quiet, very low note.

7. Continue playing until your air runs out.

8. Play down chromatically, using full air (but not loud sound) on each note of the chromatic series: 0, 2, 1, 1-2, 2-3, etc.)

You'll note a tingling, perhaps itching feeling in your lips and face, rather like that you've experienced when blood begins to flow back into an arm or leg that has fallen asleep.

If at any time you feel a "stinging" sensation, STOP IMMEDIATELY! You have blown too hard, too loudly, and to continue could cause a pressure blister inside your lip!

A great advantage to using the double-low pedals on a regular basis is that they help to "energize" your Anchor Spot^{TM} and prepare it to respond while playing. After playing the double-low pedals, try tapping lightly on your anchor spot. It should feel almost like tapping gently on your funny bone: a little tingly and a little ticklish. One of my adult, "Comeback" students refers to this as a "Lip-Gasm." Call it what you will, it is a good indicator of your readiness to play with heightened sensitivity.

This may take time to develop, especially if you've been a pressure player who is unaccustomed to feeling subtle sensations in your lips.

But after a while, you'll notice a lot more control of the finer points of articulation, tone quality, and dynamics.

In fact, another good test of your improved lip responsiveness is the "Blip Buzz." This is a very quiet, gentle buzz performed by simply closing your lips (with your teeth open, of course!) and using an air attack to begin the vibration.

If you've softened your lips sufficiently, the response should be immediate and you should be able to change pitch easily.

One final thought: using a soft center to your lips helps ensure that they do not become toughened by the playing process. In fact, you'll find that the red (both inner and outer) of your lip will feel even softer after you finish playing!

Enjoy the process!

CHAPTER 5
Well, Shut My Mouth- <u>*NOT*</u>!

Ever sit in a traffic jam for hours at a time? Even when you're doing your best to remain relaxed, the tension starts to creep in. First your hands tighten up on the wheel, then your shoulders, your neck, your back. Eventually you realize your teeth are clamped and maybe even grinding against each other. Your head begins to ache and throb and you'd like to <expletives deleted> the next car that cuts in front of you!

Sadly, many trumpet players do the equivalent of this whenever they play. Their back teeth are shut (or close to it). They rely on tongue level to change partials because their lips are flaccid (loose) in the center. Their corners are clamped tightly. The only way they can maintain a sound is to over blow and squeeze the mouthpiece against their lips so hard that the lip membrane becomes as thin (and weak) as a slice of prosciuto in a bone and metal sandwich!

It doesn't have to be this way!

Opening the back molars accomplishes several things:

1. Allows for more sound resonance by creating a larger oral cavity.
2. Forces the use of the mentalis (chin) muscles to support the embouchure.
3. Improves flexibility.
4. Increases dynamic range.
5. Enables greater variety of producible timbres (tone qualities).
6. Forces use of bottom lip roll thus creating a better seal between upper and lower lips.
7. Reduces reliance on excess pressure for playing.

For many years I played without even paying any attention to the size of my oral cavity, nor to the opening between my teeth. Then one day I had a student whose sound was SO tight and inflexible that I <u>had</u> to discover a way to assist him to relax.

I took a piece of paper, folded it into increasingly smaller squares, and had him insert it between his back molars before wetting and closing his lips.

His sound became fluid and open. His range and flexibility improved and I began seriously to consider oral cavities as an integral part of trumpet playing.

Although I believe it is important to keep the lips gently closed when playing, I have come to be a strong advocate for keeping the <u>jaw</u> open.

Relaxation can be practiced and learned systematically.

You can learn to open your jaw, relax your corners, and use the smaller muscles of a centralized embouchure to play with a freer tone quality, greater endurance, increased range and more delicacy of control.

If you have always played with tension, it may feel strange, at first, to play without it. Many of my students describe the sensation as feeling "like I'm not playing at all!"

And yet the responsiveness of their lips amazes them!

In Chapter 4 (Keep It Soft and Supple), I talked about double-low pedal tones (which help to soften and limber the lip membrane/vibrating tissues and prepare the muscles to play).

The process of playing pedals is enhanced with a relaxed jaw.

Let me clarify the issue a bit here: When you DROP your jaw, it naturally moves SLIGHTLY forward.

The issue that has brought a number of trumpeters to me with jaw issues is that of THRUSTING the lower jaw forward!(Too far for their natural anatomy)

It's a matter of degree.

For example: it is necessary to use sufficient pressure to maintain a seal between the lips, and between the lips and the mouthpiece, dependent upon dynamics and tessitura (High range).

Use of TOO MUCH pressure leads to swelling and injury, and can eventually cause (worst case scenario) the development of a cyst on the upper lip, or other pathology.

Also, "alignment of the front teeth" (by thrusting the lower jaw forward) can lead to closure of the jaw, which reduces the oral resonance cavity, reduces the area of the lips that is free to vibrate, reduces sensitivity of the lip, and can inhibit the versatility of tonguing styles available (not to mention variety of timbres).

For those of you, who'd like to experiment a bit, try the following:

1. Close your lips without moving your jaw.
2. Now, with your lips closed (and remaining closed) cause your bottom teeth to gently slide down the inside of your bottom lip as far as possible.

   You may not be able to go very far at first but, with gentle practice, you'll gradually increase the distance between your lowered bottom teeth and the place where your lips meet.

3. Now, with lips closed and teeth as far apart as possible, buzz your lips (any pitch is fine).

   If it helps, let the tip of your tongue gently touch the inside of your bottom lip about half way between where the lips meet and where the bottom teeth lie.

Most people will find that the pitch rises when you add the tongue tip.

By bringing the tongue tip downward or upward you can alter the pitch and the timbre (sound quality) of the buzz (and of the tone on the trumpet).

This technique requires the centering of the lips (toward the rim of the mouthpiece). A too loose center (as occurs when the corners are too tight: remember, it's a matter of degree!) will result in only pedal tones, a too tight center will result in a stuffy sound.

The area of the lips within the rim should remain soft so that it can vibrate freely.

By centering slightly TOWARD the rim (but leaving the very center soft) you will develop a greater degree of control of the nuances of playing.

The difference between this setup (which is SLIGHTLY pursed, but only slightly, since the lips do not come out front, away from the teeth, as in puckering) and the "tight corners" setting is the following:

1. In the "tight corners" setting, the 'aperture" or "vibration point" (for lack of a better word, I prefer "vibrating surfaces of the meeting lips") is wide from side to side, and shallow from inside to outside.

2. In this setting (slightly centered, with the jaw dropped), the vibrating surfaces of the meeting lips are narrower from side to side, but DEEPER from inside to outside. This produces a long corridor of vibration in the lips, which produces a richer more vibrant sound as well as more finite pitch and timbre control.

Of course, every setting and technique must be adapted to the natural anatomy of each individual player. A person whose lower jaw is naturally aligned or slightly protruding will have very little difficulty aligning the front teeth to play. A person whose lower jaw recedes is more likely to struggle aligning the front teeth.

I firmly believe, though, that ALL trumpeters can benefit from learning to DROP the lower jaw (separate the back molars), and I have had students and colleagues whose bruxism and TMJ have improved as at least a corollary to learning to do so while playing.

The issue with aligning the front teeth by thrusting the lower jaw forward is several fold:

1. Thrusting the lower jaw forward creates tension in the tongue itself (test this yourself), thus limiting what you are able to do with your tongue.

2. Thrusting the lower jaw forward does not necessarily open the teeth, which leaves the oral cavity diminished in size and resonating ability.

3. Thrusting the lower jaw forward may result in a pinching of the trigeminal nerve, which can wreak havoc with other facial nerves and cause severe headaches, as well as a loss of sensation in the embouchure.

4. Using the teeth (lower especially) as an anchor for the lips tends to encourage spread chops (smile embouchure again), and a wide, shallow aperture that is less easy to control and more subject to the use of excessive pressure.

5. The strain on the TMJ may not be evident at first, sometimes it takes years to show, but it WILL show inevitably with the abuse of jutting the jaw.

On the contrary, DROPPING the jaw relaxes the TMJ, allows for a strong, centered embouchure, with a narrow but DEEP aperture tunnel which adds richness to the sound, control of timbre and dynamics and range, is less likely to fatigue, etc.

The real key is to:

1. Keep the jaw open (back teeth separated)
2. Keep lips gently closed
3. Use the natural anchor spot/angle and pivot
4. Have no resistance to the air except at the lips
5. Use the tongue to interrupt the air, not necessarily STOP it.
6. Use an anchored tongue position for most (not necessarily ALL) playing
7. Support the lower lip, where it meets the lower teeth, with the tip of the tongue.

8. Drop the lower teeth away from the edge of the lower lip, but keep the lower lip touching the upper lip (this takes development of the mentalis muscles).
9. Keep the upper lip touching the soft, wet inner surface of the lower lip, except at extreme volumes or ranges.

This keeps the lips soft and vibrating within the rim of the mpc, which is the only place that really matters to trumpet players.

Let's talk about some ways to help you experience a relaxed jaw and open oral cavity.

STAGE ONE

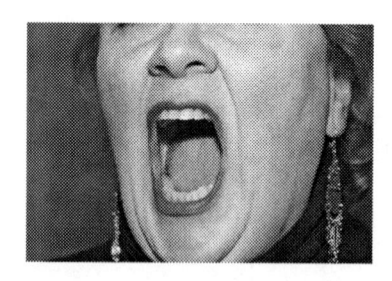

First, simply open your jaw as wide as possible,
as if yawning,
without straining.

You may wish to gently massage the outer line of your jaw from the outside of your molars up to the area in front of your ears. Just DROP your jaw: be careful to avoid thrusting it forward or backward. Merely allow it to drop. Some of you may be so tight that this will take time to achieve. A soak in a hot shower or deep bath may help before you try the next step.

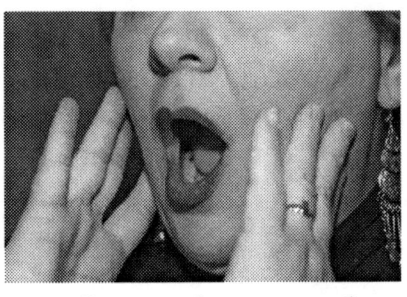

When you drop your jaw allow your lips to stay relaxed. You may notice your lower teeth dropping down, or even sliding down the inner surface of the lower lip: this is fine! Just let yourself feel the relaxation.

Now <u>gently</u> close your mouth/lips, but keep your jaw relaxed. There should be no tension or flexation in your face, simply a relaxed face, with gently touching lips.

It may help to gently roll the head around on your neck, but if you feel any tension returning STOP<!> and go back to the loose, dropped jaw.

If you've done the double-low pedal tones and gentle horse flap style buzzing, you'll be able to play gently now, even with your jaw this open. (Do be certain that you are "centralizing" your lip support!)

If you haven't done the pedals or horse flaps, I'd suggest you return to Chapter 4 (Keep It Soft and Supple) and practice the techniques described therein before proceeding.

STAGE TWO

The second stage is to make use of an insert between your back molars to <gently!> remind you to keep the jaw relaxed.

Try this: Turn your pinky finger sideways so that the nail bed faces toward your ear.

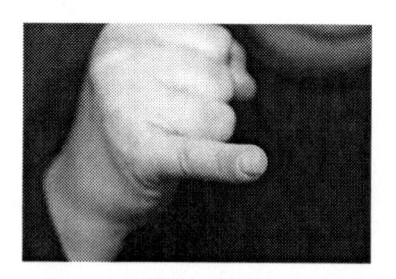

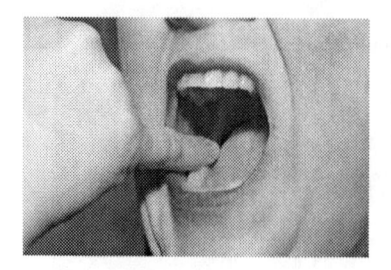

Insert the finger this way between your back molars on one side.

Gently bring your molars to meet the finger <u>without</u> clamping your jaw.

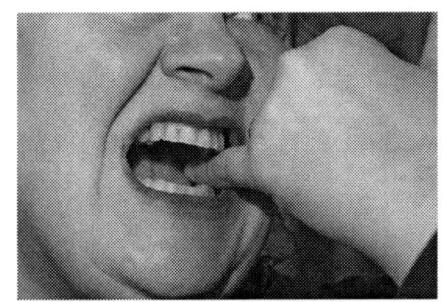

Now use your tongue tip to feel how far apart your front teeth are. For most people, the teeth will be ¼ inch to 3/8 inch apart at this point.

Next, remove the finger but keep your molars separated by the same distance.

N.B.: Be careful to avoid thrusting the jaw forward! It <u>is</u> possible to open the front teeth a bit by moving the lower jaw forward instead of down, but it sets up excess tension in the jaw and face and may lead to problems with the (TMJ) temporomandibular joint.

Now, wet and gently close your lips.

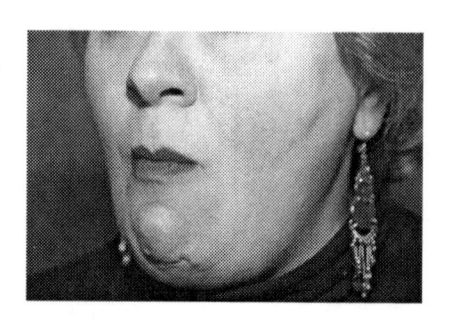

The lower lip may need to draw upward, slightly in front of the outer, lower surface of the upper teeth in order for the lips to seal. Allow it to do so.

Don't worry about "creating an aperture." The airstream will take care of this.

Place your mouthpiece on your Anchor Spot™ (see Chapter 4 for a detailed explanation of how to identify your Anchor Spot™). Breathe in through your nose and use a breath attack or tongued buzz (tip of tongue on bottom edge of top teeth) to play a note.

Don't worry about which note comes out. All you want right now is one note, not any particular note! In Chapter 6 (The Power of the Pout) we'll discuss more about how to centralize your embouchure and make optimal use of the lower lip to achieve changes in tessitura (range).

SPACERS

Some of my students have found that they achieve faster success with an open jaw by using "spacers" which are small pieces of rubber or wood placed between the back molars to remind them to keep the jaw open and relaxed. You can create "spacers" for yourself by cutting cubes from pink or gray trapezoidal pencil erasers.

> **N.B.:** Do NOT use spacers when alone! To avoid the possibility of choking, always have someone nearby who knows how to perform the Heimlich maneuver.

You can cut cubes from the erasers (I use an Exacto knife) in the following sizes:

¼ inch, 3/8 inch, ½ inch, ¾ inch.

Or for our friends across the pond:

.64 centimeters, .95 cm, 1.27 cm, 1.90 cm.

By using a cube in one side (or both sides) for 2 to 4 weeks (no more than 5 minutes at a time in the beginning), you can gradually build up the length of time you use the spacer as well as the distance your molars are separated.

Once you become proficient at the ¼ inch/ .64 cm size, move to the next larger cube and repeat the process.

Most people find they are satisfied with the 3/8 inch to ½ inch (.95 to 1.27 cm) size cube. Some like to open even wider. The largest cube with which I've been comfortable playing to high C above the staff is a 1" (2.54 cm) size cube.

It's very important to have your molars GENTLY hold the spacer. Do not "clamp" your jaw or bite down hard on the spacer: that defeats the relaxation process. Besides, it's nasty to get all those little pieces of rubber eraser in your mouth when the eraser disintegrates from your grinding your jaw!

While you are using the spacers you should practice quiet Clarke Technical Studies, Colin's or Graves' lower register flexibility studies and long tones.

Please do NOT play pedal tones with spacers in between your molars because the vibration could cause them to shake loose, causing you to swallow or choke on the rubber cube. (Again, please remember to use the spacers with a buddy nearby.)

In time you'll be able to play a full 3 octave (or greater) range with your jaw relaxed. Those who observe your playing will remark on "How easy you make it look!" and "How relaxed you are!"

Your endurance and range will improve, both in dynamic levels and tessitura; and then your sound will become full, clear, and relaxed. You'll also find greater ease of articulation (tonguing) and flexibility (lip slurs). Finally, your facility (ease of playing) and finesse (ability to play with attention to detail and nuance) will also improve.

You'll achieve so much more with so much less effort!

Enjoy the process (and the results!)

CHAPTER 6

The Power of the Pout
Developing the Lower Lip

Now that you've learned to keep your lips soft and supple and to keep your jaw open, it's time to learn some ways to fine-tune the use of your bottom lip.

The bottom lip, by virtue of its attachment to the mandible (or lower jaw) is far freer than the upper lip. This means that it can move laterally (side to side) as well as vertically (up and down).

What this means for us trumpet players is that the development and application of the lower lip in the embouchure is crucial. It also means that the set of the mouthpiece into the muscle of the upper lip needs to be low enough (without falling into the red or membrane of the upper lip) to allow for the lower lip to act freely without falling outside of the mouthpiece rim.

In Chapter 7, we'll discuss making best use of your angle and pivot to allow for the lips to move as subtly as possible, but here we'll be talking about techniques to strengthen and limber your lower lip for the best possible response.

When you were a youngster, I'm sure you made ample use of the "pout" technique: "Mo-om! Can't I stay up to watch my favorite TV show?"

(Lower lip rolled out, tears began to shine in your eyes, and SOMEtimes she gave in!)

Some of you perhaps even used an outward pout of the lower lip as you were concentrating on homework, or chewing on the end of a pencil.

Now, of course, you probably seldom, if ever, make use of a pout. (Unless, of course, you're trying to manipulate someone into indulging you!)

I'd like to suggest that you rediscover the use of a pout, but this time use it in relation to trumpet playing.

Remember that the aperture is the opening between the lips, caused by the air passing through the lips. You cannot control the aperture as such, but CAN control the muscles surrounding it (the trumpet player's *ligature*, if you will), as well as the VOLUME (quantity) and VELOCITY (speed) of your airstream.

It's important to remember that you cannot control the center of your lips by tightening the corners of your mouth. It's not physically possible.

Muscle groups in the body work in opposition to each other: if you flex the triceps muscle, the biceps goes slack; if you flex the biceps, the triceps goes slack.

Perhaps the most crucial muscle to the formation of a good, flexible embouchure is the ORBICULARIS ORIS muscle, which is a sphincter muscle (think of a drawstring bag or an old-fashioned camera shutter).

Opposed to the orbicularis oris are the risorius and buccinator muscles (the corner-tightening muscles used by those who use a *smile* type embouchure --- Note: many trumpeters who believe they do not use a *smile* system are still drawing away from the mouthpiece and tightening the corners as they ascend.)

If one flexes the corners of the lips, the center of the lips grows weak and cannot efficiently resist the airstream.

Try it: tighten your corners and use the tip of a finger to push apart the center of the lips (while you are trying to hold the lips closed by pressing them against each other). You'll find that it is relatively easy to do so. The air also finds this very easy, and you have little control over it with this system.

Now try this: let the corners relax (some of you will find this very difficult to do, so I'd suggest trying both of these exercises in the mirror so you're actually seeing what you are doing. Perhaps because of the fact the left side of the brain controls the right side of the face and vice versa, we often are doing exactly the opposite of what we THINK we are doing with our face).

Okay, corners relaxed? Now draw the lips **slightly** toward the center, pursing them without pushing out in front of the teeth (no fish faces, please!)

NOW compress the lips and try to pry them apart with your finger. A much more difficult task, isn't it?

You'll note that it takes less effort to compress the lips by doing this (and, in fact, flexibility exercises will become extremely easy for you once you've mastered this technique).

You'll also note that there is a softer, more flexible area in the center of the lips, which allows you more control over timbre, articulation, projection, and flexibility, in short: efficiency.

Let's try the following:

Use a mirror for this and the following isometric exercises, which you'll initially do off-horn, and eventually move to using while playing the horn.

PRIMARY PURSING

First, purse your lips as far forward as possible in front of the teeth.

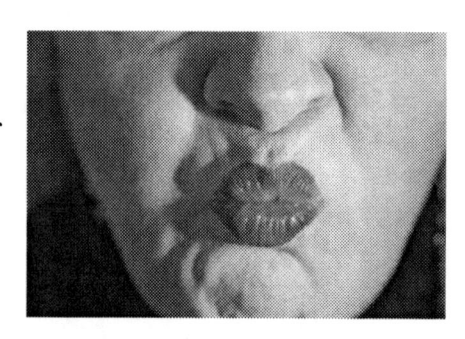

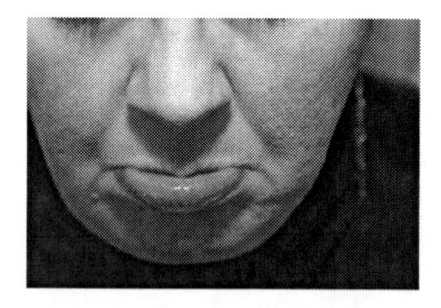

Now, slide your top lip back toward your teeth (which will cause it to move into the rolled out red membrane of the lower lip), but keep the lower lip pursed.

Practice sliding the lower lip outward (out in front of your teeth):

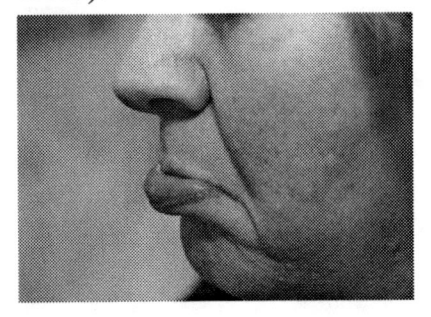

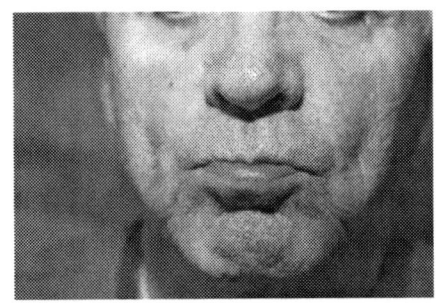

And inward (aligned with the upper lip).

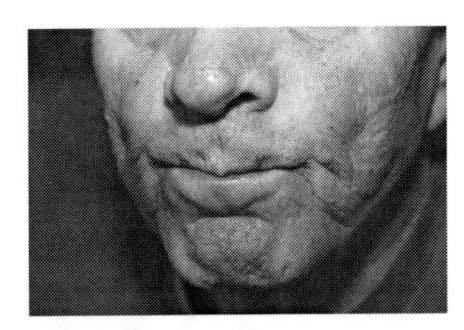

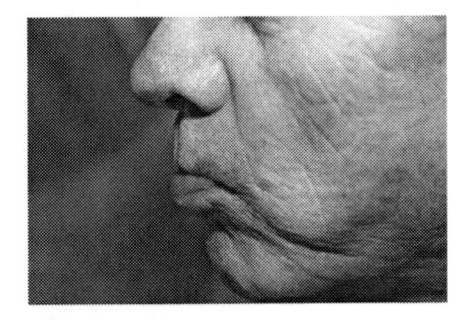

You may find that your lower lip tires quickly. Take frequent rests as you are learning to do these exercises. Over time you'll gain the ability to perform them for lengthy periods of time, but don't overdo it right now!

HMm HMm GOOD!

This exercise consists of merely holding your lips closed, as in saying the ***Hmm*** sound. When done correctly, this requires you to roll your lips slightly inward. Hold this position for as long as possible (you'll eventually be able to do it for hours at a time), until your muscles begin to burn, then rest an equivalent amount of time before repeating.

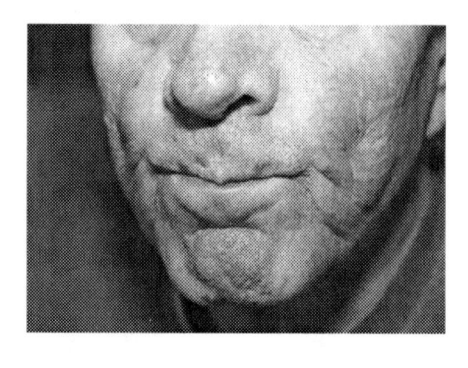

TOOTH HUGS

The second exercise is like the first, except that this time, besides the *Hmm* position, you should also draw the lip muscles in, toward the center of your lips (avoid an obvious pursing, however).

You should feel as though your lip muscles are "hugging" against your teeth. It is also important to keep the corners where they are when your mouth is relaxed while you are doing this (neither stretched outward into a "smile" nor drawn down as in a frown). Once again, hold until the muscles develop the lactic acid "burn", then release, rest, and repeat.

EXTREME MACHINE

This one is best done before a mirror, at least the first few times that you perform it, until you are sure that you are correctly performing the exercise. While observing yourself in the mirror, complete the following movements:

    a). Roll your bottom lip out and down as far as possible.(Try to touch your chin with it).

Be sure to keep the upper lip in contact with the inside of the bottom lip as you are doing this.

Hold in the extended position for a count of ten, and then gradually roll the bottom lip back up, so that it is hugging the outside of the upper lip. Rest. Repeat.

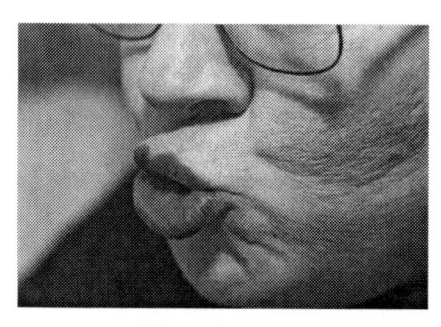

Extended Pout 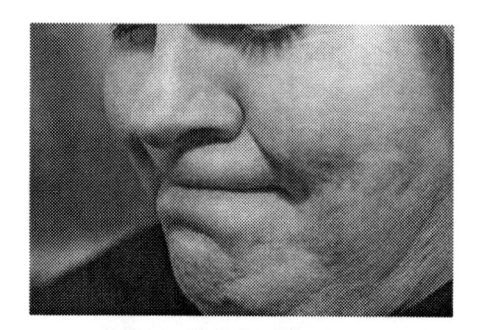   Inward Lip Hug

b). Purse your lips as far forward as possible.

First with both lips pursed:

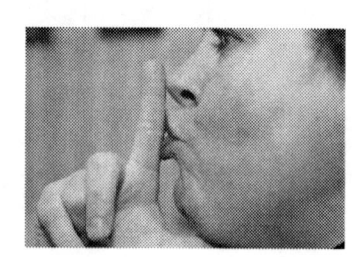

Then with only lower lip pursed). Hold for a count of ten, and then gradually relax them. Rest. Repeat.

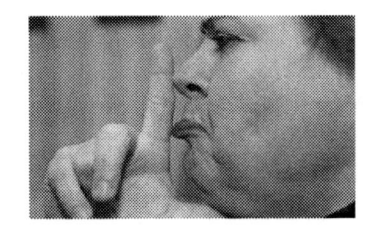

c). Roll your lips inward, so that the red (membrane) of your lips disappears. Be sure that both lips are in front of the teeth as you do this. Hold for a count of ten. Rest. Repeat.

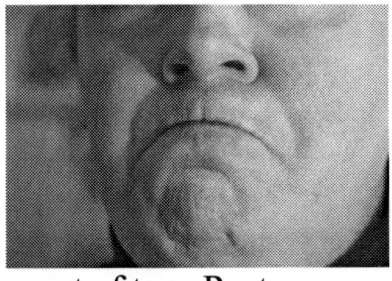

d). Flex your lips to maximum flexion. Hold for a count of 10 seconds (or as long as you can, until you feel the muscles start to "burn") Rest. Repeat.

THE PAPER CHASE

To do this you'll need to roll a square piece of paper into a tube. (Use a square that's about 4 inches by 4 inches).

Place the paper tube between your lips, but not between your teeth.

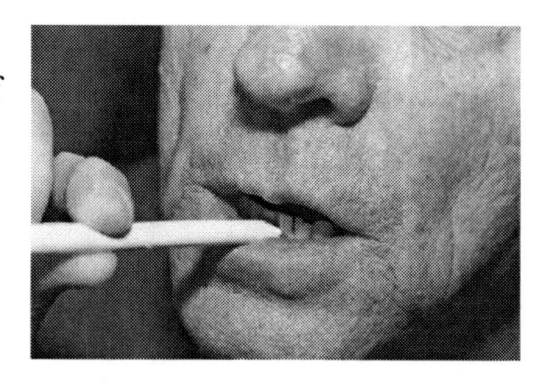

Use your lips to pivot the tube upward and downward.

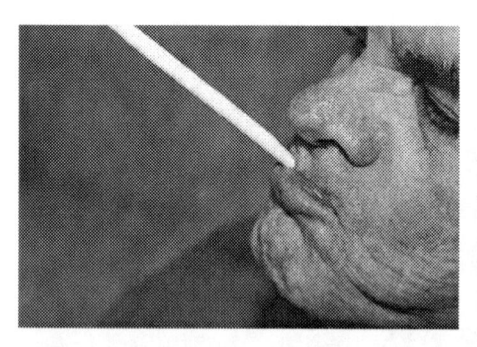

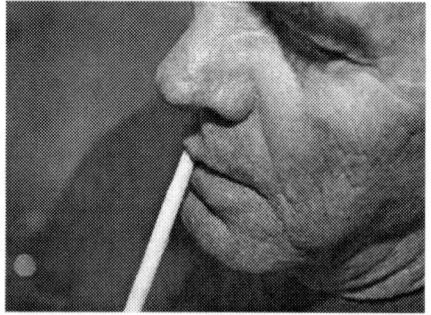

With practice, you'll eventually be able to do this with a pencil or pen. (or even a mouthpiece, by holding the mouthpiece shank between your lips. This won't happen for quite a while, so be patient!)

There is a commercial product, called "Chop-Sticks™" which has been developed by Julie Patton, of Liemar Technologies. Here is a link to her website: (copy into your browser window)

http://www.liemartech.com/Chop-Sticks/

KNUCKLE KNIBBLE (Nibble)
Use your lips (in front of your teeth) to "nibble" at the loose skin on the back of your knuckle.

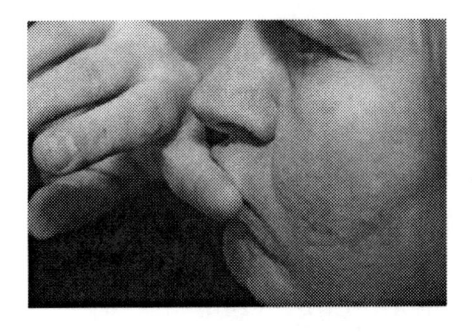

Grab knuckle skin with lips. 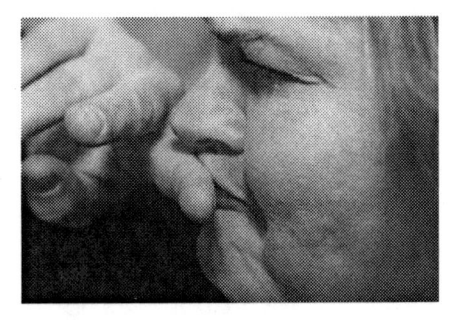   **Flex chops and pull at skin.**

THE FAMOUS SQUAWK™

My students are very familiar with the technique I refer to as the Squawk™. This consists of a very short air attacked free-buzz with a tongue-closed release. Some folks think it sounds more like a duck quacking.

It can make a very loud squawking or duck quack sort of sound, and with practice, can produce a wide range with sufficient control to produce a chromatic scale.

To produce the Squawk™ follow the following steps:

1. Produce a free buzz by starting to expel air forcefully from your lungs with your lips slightly parted.

2. As you are expelling the air, close your lips together (and roll them slightly against each other) to produce a steady buzzing sound.

3. Stop the buzz (and the air) by closing your tongue against the roof of your mouth as if saying the word "HUT!"

4. By shortening the duration of the note produced, you'll begin to produce more of a quacking sort of sound. This is the Squawk™.

5. By experimenting with centering your lips and "pinching" them together you can learn to vary the pitch and dynamic levels of the notes, but should always keep them very short and pointed in sound.

The benefits of practicing the Squawk™ include better control of popped notes (those notes you have to pick off, usually after a lengthy series of rest measures, and usually in the upper-middle to upper register), more finite control of intonation, and more delicacy of attacks in general.

With practice, it's possible to play all sorts of melodies and scales this way, and it's a good way to prevent the dreaded "BRAACK" or "FRAK" attacks, since your lips become accustomed to placing pitches very accurately.

NOTE: Once the embouchure is working efficiently (greatest amount of return for the least amount of effort) it becomes possible to access the use of air to perform with seemingly effortless technique. You'll note I used the term *seemingly*. Of course, there is always effort expended to create beauty, but there needn't be anywhere NEAR the excruciating overwork many players force upon themselves.

CHAPTER 7

What's Your Angle?
Finding Your Natural Pivot and Angle

Now that you've learned to relax your hands, align your spine, soften your lips, use your Anchor Spot™, open your jaw, make use of your lower lip, and centralize your chops, what else could you <u>possibly</u> need to consider?

Let me suggest to you that you allow your horn to "breathe." ("Gee!" you're thinking "I've heard of people loving their horns, but anthropomorphism is carrying it a bit TOO far!")

Not really, just a way to think about allowing your horn to move gently as you play, rather than clenching it in a death grip.

Every trumpet player uses some sort of angle (left to right) and pivot (up to down) when they play. Either they allow the horn to move (often minutely: it's not necessary to exaggerate the motion to achieve good results) or they distort the embouchure/chops.

Allowing the horn to move protects the chops (lips) from fatigue and allows them to move as little as possible. As we discussed in Chapters 4 (K.I.S.S.) and 6 (Pout), when the embouchure is centralized it takes very little lip-to-lip compression to change partials.

Determining your natural pivot (up to down movement of the trumpet bell when changing partials/registers) and angle (left to right movement) frees your chops from excess effort.

Many players operate pivot/angle on a somewhat diagonal plane. Determining your own plane of movement will empower your efficiency as a trumpet player, thus freeing you to concentrate on the <u>musical</u> aspects of playing.

You'll likely find that you tend to exaggerate the degree of angle and pivot you use at first, but that's okay! Eventually you'll know your range of motion and what your largest and smallest degree angles are to maintain efficient performance.

Many of the players I've come across are downstream players, but the angle/pivot approach works well for upstream players as well.

RELAX YOUR "GRIP"

Probably one of the most limiting things you can do when playing your trumpet is to hold the trumpet tightly and keep it from moving as you play. This forces you to make drastic changes in your chops to change registers and often results in the application of far more pressure of the mouthpiece against the lips than is strictly necessary.

This doesn't mean that the horn has to bounce around wildly as you play! In fact, the movements are understated, the distance traveled relatively minute. Many students who observe me playing are unable to discern the movement of my horn until they place their hands directly on my instrument.

Of course, while you are learning to use the angle/pivot you might find yourself overdoing the process at first. That's only natural! Just like a beginner learning to ride a two-wheeler bicycle will exaggerate a rocking motion until they learn the correct balance, you can expect yourself to overdo the angle and pivot for a while until you fine-tune the process.

Have patience and gradually reduce the range of motion to the minimum necessary to achieve your goal.

We'll do a series of activities to help you determine your best range of motion, pivot, and angle.

UPSTREAM vs. DOWNSTREAM

So, which is it? Are you an upstream player (usually tilting the trumpet bell upward as you ascend into the higher register) or a downstream player (usually tilting the trumpet bell downward as you ascend into the higher register)? Do you get the best lip seal with your horn tilted slightly to the right or slightly to the left?

The first exercise we'll use to help you is that of free-buzzing. In other words, wet and close your lips gently (remember to keep your back molars open!), and buzz about a second line G. Place your hand about 6 inches in front of your mouth and slur up to third space C as you do so.

UPSTREAM?

If you're an upstream player you'll probably feel air projecting upward when you free buzz (buzz your lips alone, without the horn or mouthpiece). Your lower jaw may protrude outward, past your upper jaw when you are relaxed.

DOWNSTREAM?

If you're a downstream player, you'll probably feel air projecting downward when you free buzz. Your lower jaw may recede inward, inside your upper jaw when you are relaxed.

ALIGNED?

What if your jaw is relatively well-aligned when relaxed? In this case, your free-buzzed air probably projects relatively straight outward. Your upstream/downstream tendencies will be determined as you play (functionally/physiologically rather than anatomically/structurally). You may find yourself becoming either basically upstream or basically downstream in action.

The key to success with this (and every other aspect of practicing) is to be observant of yourself and of your actions. Keep a journal to track your results and your progress. The goal is to be analytical in your practicing so that you can achieve muscle memory and be intuitive in your performances!

If possible, use a video or webcam to record yourself as you play. This will give you unbiased feedback, which is always beneficial!

The next pages demonstrate some activities to assist you in determining your best angle and pivot. Remember, these are about using gentle motion and are designed to assist you with maintaining your seal as you change registers.

> I. Play a second line G at *mf*.
>
>> Make sure your lips are slightly centered toward the rim of the mouthpiece and that the mouthpiece itself sits into the lips only enough to maintain a seal between the two lips and between the mouthpiece and lips.
>>
>> Using a very gentle lip-to-lip compression by rolling your bottom lip upward toward the upper lip, move your trumpet bell slightly in the direction of your pivot* as you slur up to 3rd space C.
>>
>>> **N.B.:** Move the bell <u>downward</u>, if you are a downstream player and <u>upward</u>, if you are an upstream player. Experiment with both if you are an aligned player)
>>
>> Use an inward kick of your upper abdominal muscles if necessary.
>>
>> You may find that it is also helpful to angle the horn slightly to the left or right as you repeat the slur.

You want to experience a sort of "click" as you make the move from one partial to the next.

Keep a log or journal of your results with each approach.

II. Practice increasingly larger intervals using your new-found pivot. While you are using your pivot, systematically adjust your angle (left to right motion) by degree to find the best angle to add to your pivot in each register or with each sort of technique.

The Ripples in the Diagnostic Daily ChopCheck™ are extremely beneficial in developing facility in using your pivot and angle.

Be careful to avoid applying pressure as you ascend through the registers, though, or you will negate the action of the lower lip.

III. Practice arpeggios using your pivot and angle. Be sure to incorporate slurs, single tonguing, double tonguing and triple tonguing as you play the arpeggios at faster tempos, always making using of your angle and pivot in the process.

Etudes such as Arban's Characteristic Study Numbers 6 and 13, and Brandt Orchestral Study #31 are particularly helpful in practicing your angle and pivot.

While you are playing them, strive to keep your head and embouchure as still as possible. Let your horn perform most of the motion. As you become more adept at using your pivot and angle experiment with reducing the degree of movement you require playing various figures.

Eventually you may find that though <u>you</u> are aware of using the angle/pivot, most folks who observe your performance will not be aware that they exist.

That's when your performance becomes perceived by the audience as being "effortless."

And <u>THAT's</u> success!

CHAPTER 8

To Buzz, Or Not to Buzz
That's the Question!

Every one of us, I suspect, began playing the trumpet by hearing some version of the following: "Wet your lips. Blow air through them to create a buzz."

Even some advanced players still believe it is necessary to be buzzing strongly before adding the mouthpiece to the embouchure. They will even go so far as to start the lips buzzing, then add the mouthpiece to buzzing lips, claiming a deficiency if the same pitch is not maintained between the buzzing lips and the buzzing mouthpiece.

Well, in the words of Sportin' Life (from <u>Porgy and Bess</u>) "It ain't necessarily so!"

Now, I'm *not* saying that early beginners won't benefit from starting out this way, because vibrating lips are not a natural state of being for the average lips! Beginners, and those who've suffered from lip injuries resulting in stiffening of the lips, can definitely benefit from buzzing AS AN ETUDE!

That's right: as an ETUDE or exercise, not as a constant way of playing.

Now before you fly off the handle and start citing exceptions, let's think about the impetus required to begin the sound on the trumpet.

ALL that is required to start a sound on the trumpet is the disturbance of the standing column of air within the horn. The simplest manifestation of this is to place the mouthpiece into the horn and tap the mouthpiece by cupping the palm over the mouthpiece (do so gently, please, or you'll need to have your mouthpiece pulled by your repair person (or by a "Bobcat" mouthpiece puller, which should be a staple in every trumpet teacher's gig bag, imho!)).

By so doing while you press the valves in a chromatic sequence, you can hear actual pitch changes in the horn.
Now, your palm isn't even capable of buzzing and yet it was able to produce pitches from the horn!

Why? If you need to know the specific physics concepts, I encourage you to talk to Nick Drozdoff (both an excellent trumpet and a dedicated science teacher) or another physics-minded genius.

For our purposes, it should be sufficient to note that the percussion of the palm striking the mouthpiece cup sends some sort of wave of vibration (if you will) into motion within the instrument.

In other words, all it takes to begin a pitch on the trumpet is some sort of disturbance of that standing column of air within the instrument.

We don't even necessarily have to use our tongue to begin a note: a simple breath attack will suffice *IF OUR LIPS ARE SOFT AND SUPPLE ENOUGH TO VIBRATE*!

In Chapter 4, Keep it Soft and Supple (KISS), we talked about ways to keep the lips soft and supple enough to vibrate well. The "Blip Buzz" is an excellent way to test the softness and suppleness (vibrate-ability) of your lips. If your lips do not vibrate as soon as you wet, close, and blow through them, you need to practice more of the double-low pedal tones to soften and limber them. In the next chapter, Chapter 11, the Daily Diagnostic CHOPCHECK™, will help identify your readiness to move on from the double-low pedals into the rest of your warmup and practice or performance.

Okay. So when IS it appropriate to make use of free and mouthpiece buzzing?

Anytime, actually, as long as you're not buzzing so loudly as to induce excess toughening of the lip tissue!

Toughening of the lip tissue?!!?? What the HECK are you talking about?

It's simple, really. Ever develop a callus on your hand from doing hard work in the yard, or perhaps putting together a piece of pre-fabricated furniture?

What happens in your skin to create a callus is called sometimes referred to as "cornification," although that term more properly refers to the development of nails. In effect, the skin thickens and hardens in response to repeated "insult" or rubbing against a hard surface. In a worst case scenario, the skin can develop into a "corn" as is sometimes seen in overlapping toes, or on the bottom of the feet due to ill-fitting shoes. Corns are usually cone-shaped, with the pointed surface extending down, into the deeper tissue, and are often surrounded by reddened, irritated skin. Calluses usually involve only the outermost layer of skin, and usually disappear when the source of irritation is lessened or removed.

This can happen with trumpet players, even in the lip tissue, with over-blowing.

Think of it this way: by over-blowing, you are forcing the lips to impact against both the hard surface of the mouthpiece AND the hard surface of your teeth. This is what causes the "stinging" sensation you feel when you

blow too hard. It can lead to pressure blisters, canker sores, and even cysts on the lips.

Many years ago, when I did a period of time on the road with the Beatty Cole Circus, I developed a sort of callus on my upper lip that took several weeks to wear off after I got home (and back to normal playing and practicing).

At that time, the first trumpet book in the circus band was not traded off and featured a lot of loud, upper register blowing. In fact, I took the place of a trumpet player who had injured his lip and had to take some time off.

USING PROPER BUZZING TECHNIQUE

If you've read through Chapter 6 (The Power of the Pout) and Chapter 4 (Keep It Soft and Supple), then you're familiar with the concept of setting your top lip slightly into the soft, inner red of the lower lip to achieve a good seal.

This is also crucial to good buzzing technique through the lower and middle registers of the trumpet.

As long as your teeth remain open and your lower lip stays slightly outside of your upper lip, your lips will not be subject to the kind of bruising, toughening and stiffening that occurs with loud, closed-teeth free buzzing.

ELEMENTARY BUZZING TECHNIQUES

I <u>do</u> advocate using some free buzzing with beginning trumpet players, but also teach my beginners the double low pedal tones (which should always following any free or mouthpiece buzzing exercises).

It's important to keep buzzing to short periods, especially for complete beginners and comeback players whose lips tend to be more sensitive to scarring and discomfort (and stiffening).

Here are some of the ideas I use with my beginners to help them begin to get a steady buzz:

AIRPLANE TAKEOFF

We begin this by simply wetting our lips, closing them, and allowing them to flop loosely (but not too loudly!)

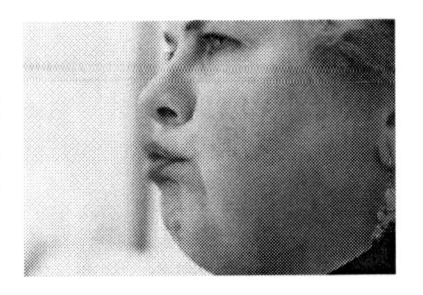

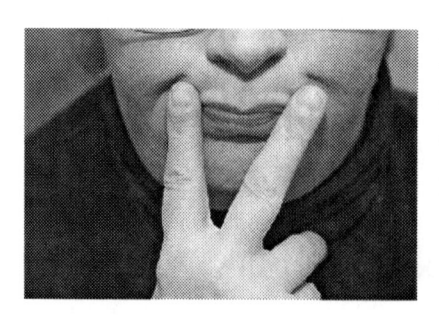

I then have the students place their fingers lightly at the sides of their lips, without pushing into the flesh at all.

As we blow slightly stronger air (using the tummy muscles, as if coughing), and close our lips slightly more, we move the fingers from the corners of the lips toward the center.

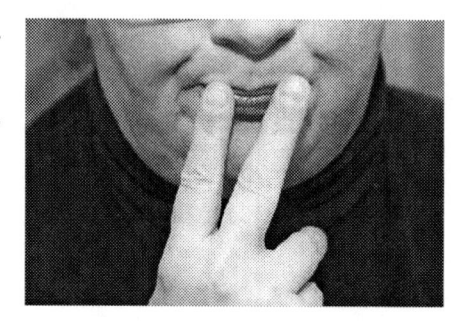

When done correctly, the buzz rises in pitch.

MOSQUITO BUZZING

For this exercise, I have the students maintain the same pitch, but increase the dynamic level by using their abdominal support (pulling IN their tummy muscles as they blow).

We often pretend we can "catch" the mosquito by clapping our hands, and then open our hands only to have the bug escape and buzz around us again.

It's one of the more popular games my younger students enjoy!

FIRE ENGINE

This is the typical rising and falling buzzing sound that imitates a fire engine. It can be done at the same dynamic level for all pitches, or can rise and fall (both in pitch and dynamics) like a Doppler effect.

Once again, I <u>always</u> follow buzzing exercises with double low pedal tones (elephant farts) to avoid stiffening of the lips, especially if continuing with a longer practice session.

For a more detailed description of buzzing, see Jim Thompson and Robert Sayer's book *Buzzing Basics* (Atlanta Brass Press, 1995) or visit Clint "Pops" McLaughlin's website: **http://www.bbtrumpet.com/**

CHAPTER 9
T^4
Terrific Tongue Technique Tips

INITIAL ATTACKS

If you were going on a trip in your car and, instead of keeping your foot steady on the gas pedal, were constantly stopping and starting the car by using the brake pedal you wouldn't get very far very fast. (And your passengers would likely be hanging their heads, and perhaps their breakfasts, out the windows!)

The same sort of idea applies to the usage of the tongue in trumpet playing. Too often I hear trumpeters who constantly use their tongues to stop every note. This interrupts the flow of the music, impedes the airstream, and generally exhausts the player's tongue long before the gig is over!

Try the following:

1. Purse your lips and blow air through them.
2. Now use your fingertip (flat) against the surface of the lip to stop the vibration.

3. Now repeat the process of pursing and blowing, but this time instead of slapping your finger tip against the lips, merely flick the fingertip through the airstream *without touching the lips at all!*

Notice how you could still hear "articulations" of the notes? That's one of the concepts I'd like to help you incorporate into your trumpet playing.

I call it "interrupting" the airstream, rather than stopping it with the tongue.

It's especially helpful for legato playing and upper register playing, but can be applied in every register and almost every style of performance.

In addition, it can help to avoid extraneous jaw movement when articulating.

In earlier chapters we talked about using the tip of the tongue to support the inside of the bottom lip. That doesn't mean that the tongue tip is unavailable for articulation, though!

By making use of the area approximately 1/8 of an inch inside from the very tip to contact the <u>bottom</u> edge of the top teeth your initial attacks will become far more secure than the traditional "tip of the tongue behind the top of the top teeth" approach.

This is because the tongue is contacting both the bottom edge of the top teeth <u>and</u> the inside of the bottom lip where it meets that bottom edge.

That's right: the bottom lip rides up, slightly over the outside of the bottom edge of the top teeth! The reason it can do this and still produce a sound is that the bottom teeth are dropped down with the open lower jaw. This creates a vibrating surface on the bottom lip that contributes to a rich, open, and vibrant sound.

The immediate impact of this is that "chirps," "fracks," and the dreaded "braack" become things of the past!

You see, when you place the tip of the tongue at the back, top edge of the top teeth you lose immediacy of attack. In other words, the air makes a sort of hiccough between the attack at the back of the top teeth and its exit at the Anchor Spot^{TM} where the lips meet.

There is also far less likelihood of delayed attack, as sometimes occurs in tense players, because the "spitting" motion of the tongue against the inside of the lips allows immediate responsive vibration of the lips (assuming that the lips are properly softened and toned via a proper CHOPCHECK™)

If any tension still remains in the player's body, it can be dissipated by the simple process of <u>swallowing</u> before releasing the air. The process of swallowing requires a relaxation of the mouth, throat, neck, and chest.

It's also important to realize that the tongue doesn't so much "attack" the notes as it does "release" them.

Let me explain:

We know, from the beginning of this chapter, that it is possible to elicit articulations from simply "interrupting" the airstream. However, it is also possible, particularly on initial attacks, to use the tongue as a valve, which simply "releases" the air by moving away from the articulation point.

Try this:

1. Make sure your lips are thoroughly wet.
2. Close your lips and take a deep breath in through your nose.
3. Set your tongue into place at the <u>top</u> edge of your top teeth.
4. Allow the air to come into your mouth from your lungs, but don't let it escape yet. Instead, let it build up behind the tongue. (Please note: I'm not asking you to stop the air at the back of your mouth or in your throat, but at the direct point where the tongue, teeth, and lips meet!)
5. Now release your tongue (drop it back down into the bottom of your mouth) to articulate the note.

You'll likely find that the attack is not as secure as you'd like and that you feel some hesitation before the lips respond.

Now try this: (Repeat the SAME process, but this time, instead of having your tongue at the top edge of your top teeth, place it at the bottom edge of your top teeth.)

1. Make sure your lips are thoroughly wet.
2. Close your lips and take a deep breath in through your nose.
3. Set your tongue into place at the <u>bottom</u> edge of your top teeth.
4. Allow the air to come into your mouth from your lungs, but don't let it escape yet. Instead, let it build up behind the tongue. (Please note: I'm not asking you to stop the air at the back of your mouth or in your throat, but at the direct point where the tongue, teeth, and lips meet!)
5. Now release your tongue (drop it back down onto the top of the bottom teeth) to articulate the note.

You're likely to find that the attack feels more secure and the lips respond more immediately.

STACCATO TONGUING

Many inexperienced trumpeters believe that "staccato" means "short" and use that belief as a justification for using a tongued release to staccato notes.

The truth is that "staccato" means literally "detached." In other words, there are spaces between staccato notes.

Using the tongue to end notes that are marked staccato, besides tiring the tongue, tends to make the notes slow and heavy in nature.

Try this:

1. Use a Metronome marking of quarter note = 120 beats per minute
2. Play four eighth notes, staccato, on a second line "G."
3. First use the syllable "Tut"
4. Now repeat the process, but this time use the syllable "TiHH" (in other words a breath release).

Notice how much lighter the notes sound with the "tihh" syllable? Now increase the metronome marking and try it again. You're likely to find that your staccato single tonguing is able to be clean at a much faster tempo than before if you were using the "tut" syllable!

MULTIPLE TONGUING

The best double-tonguers are those whose double tonguing sounds like very fast, very clean single tonguing.

Really the only way to develop that type of tonguing is to work on your "k" syllable.

Dan Patrylak, founder of the Eastman Brass Quintet, and formerly a Solo Cornetist with the USMC President's Own Band, recommends using a "Q" consonant, rather than the "k" or "g" that many people recommend.

His reasoning is this: the "q' sound happens much farther forward in your mouth than either the "ga" (very guttural, and almost into your throat) or the 'ka" (almost as far back as the "ga").

Try this: Say "queue" ("cue"), but aspirate out as you say it--rather like a little kid playing cops and robbers, pretending to shoot a gun with his finger: "Cue-Cue-Cue-Cue".

It's almost as though you're saying; "Q-hew-Q-hew-Q-hew-Q-hew", isn't it? The beauty of this is that it can be practiced both on and off the horn, so that your tongue can be worked on all day long!

Now, go to the beginning of the multiple tonguing section in the Arban's, start on an f (first space) and practice tonguing with ONLY "Q"'s at first. You want them to be very crisp: keep the length of the notes rather short, for now, so that you can concentrate on the clarity of the attack.

Once you have the entire exercise down on "Q's", add the "t" in, but not as 'TQTQ." First you should practice the pattern as "QTQT", and remember to keep the "Q's" aspirant, okay?

Finally, once you've conquered the "QTQT" to the point where IT is clear, you can move on to the "T-Q-T-Q" traditional pattern.

Another thing that may help you is to remember that Arban's "u" was the French "u," which was pronounced as "ee" with the lips pursed as if saying "oo" and gives you a better idea of the shape of the tongue.

Once again, as with the staccato tonguing technique, focus on allowing the tongue to simply "interrupt" the air, rather than trying to stop it completely. That way, your tongue "bounces" or "rides" the airstream rather than acting as a linebacker!

You might also find some success by simultaneously making use of the anchor tongue technique.

ANCHOR TONGUING

Anchor tonguing is an approach that sets (anchors) the tongue in a stationary place in the mouth (usually atop the bottom teeth) and uses a different spot for articulation.

It is very helpful with multiple tonguing and can also be used when "doodle" tonguing (very fast, legato/tenuto tonguing style used in bop and other forms of jazz).

When the area just under the tip of the tongue (and slightly inside of the tip) is rested on top of the bottom teeth, the tip of the tongue is free to support the inside of the bottom lip (thus ensuring the pitch stays constant after the attack). The area on the top of the tongue is what contacts the bottom of the top teeth for the "T" syllable (or the "Doo" syllable in doodle tonguing).

This allows the top of the tongue, just behind the top teeth to create the "Q" or "dle" syllable for the second half of the tonguing pattern.

The advantage to this far forward placement of the syllables is an increase in speed and consistency from the traditional back of the throat placement.

Another way to think about this is that the whole process closer to the very front of the mouth, so that the tongue is actually more or less rocking between the bottom and top teeth.

It takes some time, but eventually you'll find that you're able to simply rock the front of the tongue back and forth and have a very fast, very clear double tongue (which sounds like single tonguing). You'll also be able to do this at very slow speeds as well, so when you accelerate, it sounds like you're single tonguing very fast indeed.

The truth, though, is that you're doing this doodle type of double tonguing, not single tonguing which requires a separate stroke of the tongue for every single note.

ALTERNATIVE ANCHOR SPOT LOCATION

There is another possible anchor spot for the tongue that some players are able to use.

This consists of anchoring one side of the top of the tongue against the hard palate on one side of the roof of the mouth. The advantage to this is that it frees the tip of the tongue for more subtle variations of attacks.

With practice, it can become as fast as the front anchor position (and can perform a sort of tremolo tonguing even better than the forward anchor tongue position.)

It can also be helpful in situations when a trumpeter is recovering from a stroke or mild case of Bell's palsy.

TONGUE LEVELS & SYLLABLE USAGE

Because I advocate playing with the jaw very open, I generally don't advocate using the syllable "EEE" for playing higher notes. Let me repeat that: "I AM NOT AN ADVOCATE OF USING THE SYLLABLE 'EEE" FOR PLAYING HIGHER NOTES!"

That said, the reason for not so doing involves the anatomy of the soft palate at the back of the oral cavity and the entrances into the nasal sinuses, which drain into the throat.

Every person's oral cavity, like every person's lip, teeth, or tongue formation is slightly different, so there needs to be some sort of modification of any system of teaching to adapt it to the individual player. That said, there might be some persons with an exceptionally high arch to their oral cavity for whom the tongue arch, as in saying "ee", would not be a problem..

This can be noticed with certain singers as well and will reflect in their choices of head versus chest tones in various registers.

The difficulty I've observed is that players who use the "eee" arch to play into the higher register often seem to have problems with head-rushes, sometimes even to the point of nearly blacking out on the bandstand.

Now there are some who will, no doubt, disagree with me on this, but I believe that the cause of such head rushes is the uncontrolled force of misdirected airstream, which is channeling up, into the nasal sinuses, rather than out, through the lips and into the horn.

Part of my justification for this idea is the existence of some players who experience "nasal leakage" of air while they are playing.

If you examine the interior of the mouth (Go ahead and check your own right now), you'll notice that the hard palate starts at the back top of your top front teeth and extends back, arching across the roof of your mouth, until it meets a spot which is far softer. This is the soft palate, which is where, pardon the indelicacy, those who "hawk" on the sidewalk collect their ammunition.

If you arch the back of your tongue, as in saying "eee," the air will come up from your lungs, meet the tongue muscle, which is stronger than the soft palate, and be misdirected up into the extremely delicate nasal sinuses, which can be injured by the force of the air and even hemorrhage from the process.

If, however, you bring the tongue farther forward, as if saying the French sound of "eu" (in other words, think of pronouncing "ee" while forming your mouth into the shape for the "oo" sound), the arch of the tongue is brought into the "cathedral ceiling" area, if you will, of the <u>hard</u> palate.

Thus, when the air meets the tongue it will seek a softer surface, bounce against the hard palate, and back against the tongue before being directed out (along the line of the downward sloping front of the hard palate) and through the lips and into the horn.

Where this system will probably not apply is with someone who has an extremely low arch to their upper palate, in which case I believe that any tongue arch is best avoided.

As far as whistling is concerned, it isn't so much the tongue level that applies as the usage of the orbicularis oris muscle (which will become fatigued after long periods of whistling or playing).

Of course, higher notes do not require a greater volume (quantity) of air, but a greater **velocity** (speed) of air. Now this speed of air, granted, may be caused by the compression of the lips at the "aperture" or by the use of abdominal, chest, or back muscles, as in the "wedge." None-the-less, it is necessary to produce higher pitches.

The HISS TECHNIQUE

One technique that may be useful for you is that of bringing the forward section of the tongue against the back of the front teeth (or even the very front of the hard palate) to produce a sort of "hissing" airstream for a very vibrant higher register sound.

It's important when doing this to be sure to keep the jaw open and to keep the back of the tongue as far down in the mouth as possible so that you don't inadvertently apply an "ee" syllable!

THE OPEN-JAWED TRUMPETER'S "SECRET WEAPON"

Well, actually, I wouldn't really call it a "secret weapon," but the SCOOP^{TM} IS a pretty useful tool to add to your box.

What it does is give you the advantages of a "hiss" or arched tongue without impeding your airflow.

And while it will work with players who close their jaws, it's no where near as effective as it is for those of us who keep our jaws open while playing.

Here's the process:

1. Roll your tongue into a "U" shape, with the center down and the sides up. If you cannot do this, don't feel bad, because it is a genetically determined ability.
2. By keeping this shape inside your mouth while playing, you will be able to support the inner bottom lip but also provide more air compression using the sides of your tongue against the insides of your dental arch.

I find that this technique is helpful with the use of the "bubble" technique, circular breathing, and also when the lips are fatigued.

BRUSH STROKES

Another technique that I use is what I call the "brush stroke." This consists of not using a firm, or pointed tongue (as in so many types of tonguing), but more of a sweeping motion of the tongue.

It can be applied to the inside of the lips or the bottom edge of the top teeth. It can be swept from side to side, in to out (or out to in), or vertically. It provides a slightly more subtle beginning to notes, either individually or in groups. Think of applying paint with a brush, and then use your tongue as if it were a brush.

The best advice I can give you about developing your collection of tonguing techniques is to experiment in your practicing. You will be able to find many more applications for tonguing as you try new ideas.

Ta-tah for now!

CHAPTER 10

HOLD THAT TIGER!
Harnessing Air Power

Trumpet players are always concerned about using enough air, when in fact many use far too much air for the given phrase or their particular instrument or embouchure.

I used to think that you could never use enough air. I worked with other brass players to develop and measure lung capacity (and as a youngster could out-perform many of the tuba players in my music school when it came to the use of spirometers!).

Then I injured my lungs while moonlighting as a security person in a chemical factory. I had taken the job because it was a third shift job I could work after evening classical gigs or rehearsals. Babysitting was cheap (my roommate was able to take care of my son as he slept), and the bosses didn't mind if I practiced in between my key tours of the facility as long as I watched the monitors and answered any phone calls that came in.

One night the unexpected happened: I started off on my first key tour of the night. (A key tour, for those of you who've never worked in security, consists of walking around a facility with a clock into which you put keys that have been hung at various locations around the facility. The clock prints the time of the key turning onto a strip to prove that every spot that needed monitoring was, in fact, inspected during the guard's tour of duty).

I walked into the second building on the lot, entered the laboratory, took a breath, and began to choke.

Someone had failed to secure a bottle of a chemical, which was dripping onto something else that released toxic fumes.

The first feeling was that of a head rush, then a serious burning in my chest, and then I became seriously disoriented.

I continued on, into the next building where I knew a friend was working on a cleaning crew. She helped me back to the main office, where we called my boss.

A trip to the hospital showed a deficit in blood oxygen, and repeated trips to pulmonologists resulted in a diagnosis of "toxic inhalation". I was left with chronic asthma and scarring in my lungs.

I consulted a lawyer. He advised me that my case could be worth millions of dollars. "Of course, you'll have to *never play the trumpet again* so we can claim a promising career nipped in the bud!"

Never play trumpet again? *NEVER?!!!???*

Those who know me know that thought could not be even a remote possibility. Ever!
It took months and months of hard work to regain enough use of my lungs so that I could play again, and many more years to be able to play phrases of satisfying lengths, but I persevered.

Jerome Callet was an incredible comfort to me during these months. I had been introduced to Callet by my dear friend and mentor, Dr. Charles Colin (of the New York Brass Conference for Scholarships and Charles Colin Music Publishing).

Jerry even designed a special mouthpiece to assist me, his "Solo" mouthpiece, which allowed me to continue to play without using the volume of air required by my Bach 1B with a "22" throat.

The moral of this story is that I discovered that it IS possible to play with a reduced lung capacity.

Today, with management of my asthma and careful attention to my "peak flow meter" (a device that measures an asthmatics ability to empty their lungs) I manage pretty well.

But I still don't have the same lung capacity that I had pre-accident.

What to do?

If you've ever hear the expression "Work smarter, not harder" you'll be able to understand the process I began.

With Callet's help, I learned to use the muscles of my lower back and upper abdomen to support the air stream and to assist with emptying my lungs better. I also learned never to empty my lungs completely or I'd risk an asthma attack.

This required looking ahead in music, to plan my phrasing and breathing carefully. Sometimes I've had to leave out a note or two, or ask a colleague to cover a particular phrase for me. It has also required developing an ability to breathe in more slowly.

Rather than taking a quick "gasp" of air, I make a point of breathing smoothly and fully. Philip LaNormandin, a brass enthusiast for all of his 97 years of life, shared one idea with me that he found useful: When you breathe in, drop your jaw and form your mouth as if you were saying the word "Home" with a very long "O" sound. This fills your lungs deeply without creating any tension in the body. You want to feel your back expand as you inhale. Think of "spreading your wings" (your shoulder blades separating as you inhale).

There is an excellent book that introduces the Japanese concept of "Hara" (see the Bibliography for further information).

The advantage to all of this is that I've learned to make use of air SPEED (or velocity) rather than relying on air quantity (or volume), and to cultivate a completely relaxed upper body (no tension between the base of the sternum and the lips themselves).

Let me explain:

For years I'd heard people say "use more air!" to trumpeters who were struggling to reach higher notes. The trumpeters would try to do just that and their chops would collapse into a fuzzy sound, or they would feel a sharp pain in their lips and suddenly be unable to play for days at a time.

Now, with Jerry Callet's help, I began to explore air SPEED as the factor in changing registers.

Allowing a greater volume of air to flow in lower register playing (but at a slower speed) created a rich, warm sound that was easier to control for articulation, dynamics, and timbre (sound quality).

Using a faster speed of air in the upper register created a vibrant, free-flowing sound that could be darkened or lightened using lip roll and tongue shape within the oral cavity, and articulation in the upper register ceased to be a concern as well.

Lucas Spiros, solo euphonium player in the USMC (President's Own Marine Band), recommends keeping the chest expanded during and after exhalation. This allows you to refill your lungs with less physical exertion and greater speed than collapsing and re-expanding with every breath.

Bobby Shew describes breath support as the "Wedge". Much like the bellows used with a fireplace, the wedge support system consists of engaging the lower back muscles (a feeling like sitting the shoulder blades down, toward the waist in the back), and the upper abdominal muscles (a feeling like coughing or retching so that the stomach moves inward strongly) to help compress and focus the air.

It is important to remember, however, that not all playing or registers require use of the wedge! Playing at mezzo forte (medium loud) in the middle register does not require as strong support as playing loudly in the upper register or very softly in the lower register.

That's right: you must use extra support to produce a good quality sound in the lower register, particularly at very quiet dynamic levels.

For some, simply thinking about breathing into the base of your spine may help you to take a deep, relaxed breath.

Another concept that has proved to be helpful is that of maintaining a "bubble" of air within the oral cavity while playing.

> **N.B.**: This idea really doesn't work well if you are using very tight corners or a "smile" type of embouchure!

The "bubble" helps to provide roundness to your sound, helps to keep the cheeks relatively relaxed and enhances the use of the centered embouchure by helping to keep air pressure consistent within the mouth.

It does NOT lead to a closed throat or the Valsalva maneuver, because you are not impeding the flow of air from the lungs, merely allowing that air to circulate within the oral cavity.

To make the best use of this, your jaw must be open (see Chapter 5), your tongue tip forward, and your lips closed (see Chapters 4 & 9).

It might help to temporarily allow your cheeks to "puff" slightly as you try this.

Try the following in your practice routine for the next week and see what it does for your sound, endurance, and phrasing:

AIR BUBBLE TECHNIQUE

1. Make sure your lips are wet.

2. Make sure your teeth (molars) are wide open.

3. Breathe deeply (as if saying the word "HOME" with a very long "O")

4. Close your lips gently, keeping them soft in the center.

5. Use a breath attack to begin a note.

6. Experiment with applying lip vibrato, gentle legato tonguing, or lip roll. Thinking about the inner-to-outer depth or thickness of the pucker may help you to better understand the easy, subtle adjustments that are possible when making use of the "bubble."

7. Also experiment with various types of tonguing, and in different registers.

With a little practice you'll find that this technique adds to your palette of techniques, of tone colors and of articulations. (See Chapter 17)

A final note on breathing: it is important to breathe always FOR THE PHRASE you must play! Too often trumpeters take a fast, inadequate breath that leaves them without sufficient air to complete a phrase. Some, alternatively, will take in too much air for the phrase and find that they must expel stale air before taking a fresh breath.

Breathe enough air for the phrase you must play, but just <u>enough</u> air. This will take experimentation on your part: no teacher can tell you exactly how much air you will or won't need for a particular phrase, only experience! With time and practice, though, you'll become an expert at playing beautiful phrases with good sound, nuance and articulation.

Now go practice!

Chapter 11

The Daily Diagnostic CHOPCHECK™
Creating and Using a Daily Practice Routine

What would you think if I told you that there is the equivalent of a GPS system to help trumpet players navigate their way through their performance day?

So many trumpet players spend unnecessary hours trying to find their "sweet spot" and rediscover how to get their lips functioning. And they do this, over and over again, every day!

It doesn't have to be that way!

By making use of the Daily Diagnostic CHOPCHECK™ (see Appendix IV), you can have feedback about your chops and develop the kind of consistency you've always wanted by making use of a reliable feedback loop *in your daily warmup routine*!

Each step of the Daily Diagnostic CHOPCHECK™ is designed to test your readiness to move on to the next step.

When you have completed the full CHOPCHECK™ you will be ready for your daily practice routine or performance. There is no more worrying about "finding" your chops, instead you will recreate them, efficiently, every time you play, by performing at least an abbreviated CHOPCHECK™ every time you are away from the horn for twenty minutes or more.

PREPARING FOR THE CHOPCHECK™

Please be aware that the CHOPCHECK™ should not be considered to be "practice" as such (since practice may be seen as something that is done when the time is available), but as a necessary part of your daily life, much the same as brushing your teeth, washing your face, and the like.

No approach to playing will ever work for you until and unless you are willing to commit yourself to a certain amount of time every day. I'd suggest that you plan your routine for rather early in the day, if possible. That way, should distractions occur, you will have already accomplished a major goal for yourself (every day).

Accomplishing a major goal (completing your routine) on a daily basis will do more than improve your trumpet playing. It will enhance your overall self-image and self-esteem, as well as awakening your mind's abilities to function better in communication across the separate hemispheres of the brain, increase the oxygenation of your bloodstream, and help you to attain confidence and balanced relaxation throughout the rest of your day.

TOOLS NEEDED

1. A straight-backed chair, preferably with a straight seat (not slanting backwards, not slanting forwards)
2. Your main instrument (for most players, a Bb, but symphony players may wish to use their C)
3. Your standard mouthpiece (preferably one that has been properly fit to your embouchure, neither too shallow nor too deep, with a throat and backbore conducive to comfortable playing (neither too large, nor too constricting)
4. A metronome.
5. A pitcher of water and a full glass (8 oz. or bigger) of water.
6. A music stand.
7. Besides the CHOPCHECK™ you should have the following books:

    - **Arban's Complete Conservatory Method** (preferably the Fischer Ed.)
    - **Clarke's Technical Studies for Cornet/Trumpet**
    - **Colin's Lip Flexibilities** or **Graves' Fundamental Flexibilities**
    - **an Etude Book**, (i.e.: Charlier, Laurent, etc) for now we'll use Vassily Brandt's "Etudes for Trumpet" (published by MCA)

WORKING THROUGH THE Daily Diagnostic CHOPCHECK™

STEP ONE: Deep Breathing and Buzzing

1. Breathe in, slowly and fully, as though you were trying to fill your lungs to the base of your backbone. You may breathe in through your nose or your mouth, but most players find the best results from opening their mouth widely as if they were saying the word "HOME."

2. Blow the air out gently, as if sighing hard.

3. Repeat the process, but this time purse your lips as you blow out.

4. Repeat the process, but this time wet your lips and blow slow "horseflaps" through gently closed lips.

5. Repeat the process, but this time close your lips more securely and buzz a gentle second line "G."

6. Repeat the process, but this time apply the mouthpiece to your closed lips, taking care to place it onto your Anchor Spot™.

7. Finally, repeat the process, but this time do a gentle lip slur of a major third or perfect fourth.

STEP TWO: Double Low PEDAL TONES ("Elephant Farts")

1. Place your mouthpiece gently into your mouthpiece receiver, and tap it lightly so that you can hear a concert Bb.

2. Roll your lower lip outward, and touch your upper lip to the wet, inner surface of the lower lip.

3. Place the upper rim of the mouthpiece high onto your upper lip and tilt the trumpet's bell upward as you slide the mouthpiece down to your natural anchor spot. (See photos in Chapter 4)

4. Tilt the mouthpiece <u>slightly</u> down until the complete mouthpiece rim is in contact with both lips (the lower lip may sit outside the lower rim of the mouthpiece: don't be concerned about this if it happens, as long as both lips are in contact with each other and with the mouthpiece. You may need to tilt the trumpet bell up or down slightly to get the pedals to speak.

    Remember: this is not a regular embouchure setting; it's for double low pedals only!) Don't allow the mouthpiece to separate the lips, though.

5. The lower rim of the mouthpiece will actually sit INSIDE the bottom lip.

   A. Take a deep breath (through your nose) and blow <u>very</u> gently to achieve a very quiet, very low note. Be gentle during this phase of the process and you'll be more powerful than you ever thought you could be later on.

   B. Continue playing until your air runs out.

   C. Play down chromatically, using full air (but not loud sound) on each note of the chromatic series: 0, 2, 1, 1-2, 2-3, etc.)

You'll note a tingling, perhaps itching feeling in your lips and face, rather like that you've experienced when blood begins to flow back into an arm or leg that has fallen asleep. If at any time you feel a "stinging" sensation, STOP IMMEDIATELY! You have blown too hard, too loudly, and to continue could cause a pressure blister inside your lip!

There are several purposes for the double low pedals:

1. They get the air flowing.
2. They soften the lip membrane.
3. They warm the muscle tissue (to avoid injury).
4. They loosen and limber the lips and embouchure.
5. They prepare the ANCHOR SPOT™ for mouthpiece placement.
6. They prepare the lips to access the natural angle and pivot.

A great advantage to using the double-low pedals on a regular basis is that they help to "energize" your Anchor Spot™ and prepare it to respond while playing. After playing the double-low pedals, try tapping lightly on your anchor spot. It should feel almost like tapping gently on your funny bone: a little tingly and a little ticklish. One of my adult, "Comeback" students refers to this as a "Lip-Gasm." Call it what you will, it is a good indicator of your readiness to play with heightened sensitivity.

STEP THREE: LIP TONERS

Lip Toners are a combination of lip flexibilities and long tones. They are accomplished by a combination of lip purse and lip "pinch" (lip to lip compression) together with increased abdominal support (pulling inward and upward with the upper abdominal muscles, and downward and inward with the lower back muscles), and a natural pivot/angle.

> **N.B.:** Do NOT use "vibrato" on the diagnostic CHOPCHECK™ since it masks the nature of the lip function and the tone produced.

You should hear and feel a crisp "click" between partials if your lips are sufficiently energized from playing enough of the double low pedal tones.

If on any one of the Toners you fail to achieve the "click," stop and go back to playing the pedals over again.

Also, if you are unable to play a second line "G" as your first note, or you do not set for a "G" and play a low "C" after the pedals, go back and play the pedals again.

If you start by playing and setting on a low "C," you will struggle with range above the staff.

The goal of the toners is to achieve a solid "Set-point" of the octave between "G" on the staff and "G" at the top of the staff.

If you are drawing your lips into a slight "purse" (centered toward the mouthpiece rim), it will take very little of the "pinch" (lip to lip compression by upward roll of the bottom lip) to jump partials. This is also essential to the playing of the ripples later in the CHOPCHECK™.

Play each of the lip slurs with four valve combinations (Open, 2nd, 1st, and 1st & 2nd). You need not go to lower valve combinations at this stage of the process, since that would involve more resistance than is necessary at this point.

Hold the second note of each toner for the full span of your breath, without allowing your chest to collapse.

Follow the sequence shown in the TONERS section of the CHOPCHECKTM in Appendix IV, to ascend to "G" at the top of the staff.

STEP FOUR: TONGUING "Eye-blinkers"

These exercises are to be played very slowly, with a very FIRM attack and a breath release. Strive for a clear, strong attack by placing the tongue on the inside of the lower lip where it meets the bottom edge of the top teeth. After the attack, allow the tip of the tongue to rest lightly against the inner surface of the bottom lip to keep it from collapsing inward (which would make the pitch go flat).

(You should only tongue on the roof of your mouth for legato passages.)

Strive for clean, clear marcato attacks, but not long notes. It is the initial burst of air that taxes the lips the most, and will, in the long run provide you with the fastest development.

Listen carefully to your attack, and avoid any type of "chirping" sound (an unclear attack, which indicates that the tongue is not sufficiently pointed, or has slipped onto the back of the top teeth, or even to the roof of the mouth). Follow the sheet for rhythmic patterns and tessitura. Play each 2 beat section of each measure multiple times for the greatest increase in power and endurance.

T³

When you feel you have reached your limit, try three times to complete the exercise. If after 3 tries you haven't reached the note, leave it for today. It will be there next time or the time after that. Don't allow yourself to become obsessed by exercises!

STEP FIVE: LIP FLEXIBILITIES "Ripples"

At this stage, you'll see fastest results by doing the "Ripples" exercise, that is, the fast/lazy octave slurs (on the Flexibilities Studies of the CHOPCHECK™) played by hitting every harmonic in the octave in rapid succession. This is the very best way to train your bottom lip to do its job.

Repeat each "Ripple" at least three times before continuing.

Continue through succeedingly higher partials (not written, but G to G with 1/3 fingering is the next partial, B to B is the next partial, etc.) and ascend chromatically through the fingerings as you do so.

Again, when trying for higher notes, make three attempts (but do go down the chromatic fingerings: sometimes an A won't come out, but a Bb or C WILL), and then move on.

If the "Ripples" are beyond you at this point, use one of the easier flexibility studies in the Graves' or Colin books.

STEP SIX: FLOW STUDIES

Now you should be ready to continue into a flow study. Choose an etude that requires steady, consistent air flow and rapid valve work for the best results. I particularly like both page 297 (Characteristic Study No. 13) in the Arban's book and Study 31 in the Brandt Orchestral Studies book (edited by Vacchiano).

The focus of this etude is to play gently and quietly while moving your airstream. Be sure to finger the valves decisively (but do NOT "bang" them: keep the concept of moving your fingers quickly, but under water, for the smoothest action). Concentrate on "riding the airstream" THROUGH the phrases.

Short term goal: play to the first breath mark.

Long term goal: play through the entire piece.

Do use alternate fingerings where marked.

QUESTIONS AND ANSWERS ABOUT THE CHOPCHECK™

Q: What is the purpose of the CHOPCHECK™?

A: The purpose of the CHOPCHECK™ is to prepare the lips for the demands required of them in the session immediately following the CHOPCHECK™. So, for example, if you are going to be practicing rather leisurely you could take a longer time playing them. If you are going to be playing very loudly or very high you might need to do wider crescendos and or higher ripples. The whole point is for the CHOPCHECK™ to be flexible to the needs of the player, rather than being a rigid routine (which could cause anxieties when a player has less time for a CHOPCHECK™ --as sometimes happens when players who are used to a lengthy warmup have to play with little or no warmup at all and they panic). With the CHOPCHECK™, you should be able to play in as little as 2-5 minutes (sometimes even less), when necessary and then consciously focus on continuing the process during actual playing.

The other thing that the CHOPCHECK™ does is to set the body up for playing. Thus, one should always use good posture and proper hand positions (no slouching, please) either when doing the CHOPCHECK™ or when performing or practicing.

And the CHOPCHECK™ is the time to focus on breathing, muscle use, airstream focus, and other aspects of playing which should, through practice, become more automatic in performance.

Q: What are specific things to strive for in the lip-buzz?

A: There are several different ways to buzz: the "horseflap" or very slow, gentle buzz, really helps to get the blood to begin to flow into the lip tissues. The sharp "squawk" buzz is good for focusing pitch and accuracy; and the melodic buzz is good for ear training as well as strengthening the lips.

Q: What sound should one aim for when buzzing the mouthpiece?

A: It depends on the type of buzz being used: it could be slow and gentle (like a tuba note) or angry and harsh (like a bee buzzing) for the higher melodic buzz.

Q: "Elephant farts": do you advocate playing them very strong?

A: No. I don't; and the reason for that is that playing them very strongly can bruise the lips (by causing them to bang hard against the edges of the teeth and the metal of the mouthpiece). My entire focus is that of preventing injuries from occurring (though I spend much time in correcting those that have already happened). It's much like (medical analogy, again) a physician who tries to teach good nutrition and good body form to athletes to prevent injuries before they happen, but also is capable of teaching the athlete how to heal the injury if it does occur (and, by extension, teach proper position and movement to prevent recurring or future injury).

So, once again, these "elephant farts" should be very nice and loose (and slow in vibration). Their purpose is to:

   1. Get the blood flowing

   2. Get the air flowing

   3. Warm, loosen, and limber the facial muscles and

4. (When needed) Refresh (this is done by helping blood to flow through the tissues, thus washing away the by-products of metabolism, namely the ash or lactic acid that comes from burning the muscles' fuel.)

Q: Toners - what volume here, and do you emphasize air speed when shifting to the upper note?

A: Start mezzo piano to mezzo forte and crescendo, but only to forte (especially to begin with: again, we're looking to begin the process of playing, not injure delicate tissue).

And, yes, most definitely INCREASE the air speed (and the abdominal support) to change harmonics.

At first, beginners may use far too much movement of the facial muscles. That's okay: beginners at anything often tend to exaggerate (muscle control begins with larger muscles, then spreads to smaller muscles with time, and development).

Think of starting to ride a bicycle, or even writing with a pencil: at first, children use a very thick pencil, and write in very big letters; gradually they develop more control and are able to write smaller, with smaller writing utensils, and eventually learn to write in "cursive" (or sometimes even more advanced calligraphy!)

Also, you <u>do</u> want to bring the chin muscles up as you ascend (though the jaw needs to remain as open as possible). This creates the "bunched chin." Again, you are training the muscles to do the job they'll need to do when playing (which must be automatic at the point of performance). The specific muscles for the toners are mostly the "mentalis" muscles of the chin. These, when well-developed, produce a sort of triangle, with the base as the chin, and the two diagonals leading from the outsides of the chin, up, toward the center of the bottom lip.

Q: Tonguing - do you use the tip of the tongue between the teeth all the time?

A: No. I don't use the tongue between the teeth always. For example, one cannot legato tongue this way (legato must be articulated on the roof of the mouth). I do, however, insist on this process during the tonguing portion of the CHOPCHECK™. These "eyeblinkers" are part of the "lip" check more so than the "tongue" check. I believe tonguing exercises belong in the regular practice session, unless a particular passage is very difficult, in which case it gets added onto the end of the CHOPCHECK™, before the rest of practicing or performing.

The reason this is considered part of the "lip" check is that the tongue is placed on the inside of the bottom lip, where it meets the lower edge of the top teeth. This allows for tremendous pressure to build up within the oral cavity, if the player remembers to use good bodily support of the air.

When that tongue is removed, and the air is released, there is a tremendous burst of air power against the lips, which must hold strongly to keep from collapsing. Hence, a lip exercise.

Q: Is this in your opinion considered controversial, that is, have you met reaction?

A: Yes, of course, there are those who adhere to the "always touch the tip of the tongue to the back of the top teeth theory." I don't.

There are so many colours available to us as trumpeters: in timbre, in dynamics, and, yes, in articulations.

We can play very marcato attacks with abrupt releases (as should occur in these tonguing "eyeblinkers"), or at the other extreme, we can play such delicate legato with tenuto releases, that the sound is like that of a flowing stream over the stones in its bed; or any range of articulation/release in between, including double, triple, and doodle tonguing.

What a wonderful diversity! Why limit yourself to one style of tonguing? This is what separates the artists from the journeymen: attention to detail.

Back to the tonguing. For very strong, marcato attacks, it IS best to strike upon the inside of the lip--as it is for very delicate, but clear (rather than legato) attacks, especially in the very high register. At other times, of course, it is important to be able to tongue on the teeth, or the roof of the mouth, or even (for a VERY vulgar effect) through the lips themselves (though I don't recommend this for most types of playing/players at all).

It is also helpful to keep the tip of the tongue as far forward as possible after the attack (to prevent the pitch from gloing flat from the lower lip's inward collapse). This is also helpful when arching the tongue--if the arch is farther forward than the soft palate area, there is less likelihood of "headrush" occurring, since forced air is not being directed up into the delicate nasal sinuses (again, prophylaxis against injury).

Is this controversial? You tell me: Is it worthwhile to learn to play with flexibility and versatility, without the risk of injury (and the possibility of an end to playing)? I think it is.

Q: If going high (Flex no. 4) do you feel that flexibility can be better done later in practice?

A: Honestly? I usually play the ripples up to at least g''' (the g above high C above the staff) when I do my CHOPCHECK™, and generally recommend that my students play to their highest, comfortable note; and then make three attempts at the next series <u>above</u> that "comfortable" note.

ALWAYS TRY THREE TIMES! (It's a sign that's been on the walls of my studios for years along with: "I <u>CAN</u> DO IT!"). More than three tries without success, and you're starting to beat yourself up--not a good thing! Less than three tries and you're giving up too soon.

You'll be surprised at how quickly this begins to yield results!

Q: How long should one play in a typical practice day?

A: Well, for a period of about 12 years during my early years I practiced anywhere from 12-14 hours per day.

Of course, had I had the guidance of a good teacher, I probably could have accomplished the same things with fewer hours, but since I didn't know any better and was in public school with a 10-15 minute lesson with an itinerant teacher every other week, I made it a point to travel cover to cover in the Arban's book, Ernest Williams, Charles Colin, etc books, just playing and playing, then playing along with records and the radio, then practicing some more. It left me with strong chops to this day.

Do I practice that much today? No, of course not. But it doesn't take long to work up performances when you've established that sort of muscle memory from years of hard work, and usually two weeks of 2-3 hours a day will have a performance memorized and ready today.

In addition, I was playing Maurice Andre arrangements on the big Bb trumpet (in the original keys and octaves) because I didn't know what a piccolo trumpet WAS! By the time I finally got a piccolo trumpet, the chops were so strong from playing in the upper register (and the priest-organist who pushed me to perform was so insidious about my learning the repertoire) that the piccolo was easy!

I tell my students that if they want to perform for a living, at some point they must make the decision to devote 8 hours or more per day to playing their horn (not necessarily just practicing, but I include performing and rehearsing as well now that I've learned more.)

And this must continue for several years in order to create a "bank" of muscle memory from which to draw in later years.

For amateurs and comeback players (CP's) I generally recommend at least 45 minutes per day of practice, though 90 is better (more than that can be counter-productive, at least until the chops have been gradually built up some).

Once you've established some chops, a minimum of thirty minutes per day will keep the chops you have. Less than that and you might as well take the day off (unless, of course, you have time to play a daily CHOPCHECK™.)

When I started playing, at the age of 7, I played 20-30 minutes per day for the first year, an hour per day the next year, and was playing 90 minutes to 2 hours per day by the time I was nine. When I started to play in church, at age 10, I was usually practicing 3 hours per day. By the time I was 12 I was performing professionally on a regular basis and teaching adults.

So you see, for me, trumpet became my life early on. I'm not saying that this approach is for everyone, but it worked for me.

Of course, legend says that Chopin himself said "Three hours of practicing in a day is enough."

THE DAILY PRACTICE ROUTINE

Every trumpet player must develop her own practice routine, based upon personal skills, anatomical and physiological development, performance needs, etc.

In general, doing the daily diagnostic CHOPCHECK™ will set you up to continue with any playing you might have to do in a given day (the bone underlying the meat, as it were).

Then your workout or practice routine (the meat of the day) will delve into all the aspects of playing, in depth: tonguing, breathing, lip vibrations and flexibilities, scales, arpeggios, patterns, woodshedding, solo material, jazz or melodic improvisation, etc. This may be broken into two or three separate sessions, depending on your available time and what you need to develop.

The final workout of the day, after a break, should be spent working on repertoire (the skin atop the meat atop the bone).

The order in which you approach these tasks, after the CHOPCHECK™ may vary from other players, and even from day to day in your own approach, but it's important to cover a broad range of factors every day.

See the Bibliography at the back of the book for some suggested books.

SCALES PRACTICE

It goes without saying that you should play through all twelve keys of major and minor scales (in every form), 2 octaves when possible (or three, if possible). You should also be able to play chromatic scales starting on any note and ending on any note, all the way through your usable range.

Modal scales and modified scales (Yusef Lateef publishes a Compendium of Scales that includes hundreds of scales for practice) are also beneficial.

Being able to play scales well establishes good muscle memory, which will make you a better sight reader, too!

Play all your scales with a variety of rhythms and articulation patterns:

1. All single-tongued.
2. All slurred.
3. Double tongued, in sixteenths.
4. Triple tongued, in triplets
5. Slur two, tongue two (sixteenths)
6. Tongue two, slur two (16ths)
7. Slur two, tongue one (triplets)
8. Tongue one, slur two (triplets)

Repeat the process, this time playing scales in thirds, then fourths, then fifths, then turn-arounds (do-mi-re-do, re-fa-mi-re, mi-sol-fa-mi, etc) and (do-re-mi-do, re-mi-fa-re, mi-fa-sol-mi) etc.

Repeat the process with each form of the minor scales (harmonic, melodic, and natural).

The sequence of scales may be followed chromatically up or down, or via the circle of fifths (either up or down) so you needn't get bored with them.

CLARKE TECHNICAL STUDIES APPROACH

Following the scales, it's time to move onto the **Clarke Technical Studies:**

Starting with the first studies, follow this process:

1. Play all slurred.
2. Play all single tongued.
3. Play all double tongued.
4. Play all triple tongued (it changes the rhythmic figures to sextuplets, but do it anyway)
5. Slur two, tongue two, slur two.
6. Tongue two, slur two, tongue two.
7. Slur four, tongue two.
8. Tongue four, slur two.
9. Tongue one, slur two (through the rest of the exercise).
10. Tongue one, slur two, tongue one.
11. Play all "Q"s ("k"s)
12. Play "QTQT"
13. Play "QTTQTT"

Also play these up an octave where you can, using the same tonguing approach as above.

Clarke Technical Studies, 2nd Exercises:

1. Play all slurred.
2. Play all single tongued.
3. Play all double tongued.
4. Slur two, tongue two
5. Tongue two, slur two
6. Slur three, tongue one
7. Tongue four, slur two
8. Tongue one, slur two through the rest of the exercise
9. Tongue one, slur two, tongue one
10. Play all "Q'" s ("k'" s)
11. Play "QTQT"

Continue this process through the third and fourth and fifth studies as you have time (to the total time you've allotted to technical practice, which should be at least 30 minutes, but no more than 90 minutes).

Take a break equal to the time you've been practicing.

ETUDE PRACTICE

Next should be etude practice.

Choose an etude that will challenge you, but that you will be able to master in a one to two week period of time.

First, attempt to play the etude through as a sight-reading exercise.

Next, analyze the structure of the etude: note the melodic/harmonic structure, form, dynamics, articulations, phrases, etc.

Woodshed on those passages with which you struggled during the reading.

If you were able to sight-read the piece with few to no errors, you need to choose a more difficult piece.

Finally, play through the piece again, in its entirety. This time use a metronome to keep your tempo strict.

Rest for an equal period of time to that which you've played.

SOLO PRACTICE

First, you should have listened to the solo, as played by a fine player, such as Thomas Stevens, Phil Smith, Rolf Smedvig, or Maurice Andre, before starting to play the piece yourself. This is not so you imitate them, but that so you have an integrated image of the entire piece, not just the trumpet part.

Using a metronome to keep your pace steady (and it goes without saying that you should've been using a metronome to practice the technical studies), play through the first phrase of the solo, taking care to pay attention to dynamics, articulation and releases.

You want to have the air <u>flowing</u> through the musical line, whether the notes are legato, or marcato, tenuto or staccato, the music must always FLOW.

Your valves should be in sync with your tongue and your lips. There should be no **blurps** between the notes, and certainly no smears (caused by valves being pushed down too timidly). Be aware that the slightest bit of a delay between the tongue attack and the valve action can help to ensure clarity of attacks.

Pay close attention to the inner phrase of the music: let the energy increase slightly at tension points, and relax at resolutions (this comes from Renaissance period practice).

Think about the musical line:

Should there be a slight crescendo in a rising line, or a decrescendo? (Either may be valid, depending on the style and the effect desired). Answer other questions as they arise.

When you are satisfied with that first phrase, move on to the next. Follow the same process, then add the two phrases together.

Analyze the music to note high points in pitch, dynamics, tension, texture, and use those points to enhance your performance.

Continue the process through the piece or movement (this can become more specific with a particular piece in mind).

Before leaving this practice session, attempt to **perform** the piece or movement all the way through, focusing on making the performance as musically sensitive as possible (you might want to tape record this part of your practice).

FINAL SESSION

If you have time for another practice session in your day, try to spend some time playing along with favorite recordings (this is what jazz musicians call "chasing" the music).

This will help to develop your ear as well as your chops (technical and lip).

It's also a lot of fun, which is something that can be forgotten in the race to play higher, faster and louder.

You might also enjoy playing some of Rich Willey's Bop or Dixieland Duets. The sound file accompaniments are available on his website:

http://www.boptism.com

Or you may want to try playing with some Music Minus One recordings or using the Smart Music or Vivace programs (which offer accompaniments to standard repertoire).

The most important thing you can do in your practice and your playing is to enjoy the process!

CHAPTER 12

Swim through the Woodshed
Efficient Practice

Boy! Talk about mixed metaphors! How the heck can you go swimming in a woodshed?

You can't. That is, not unless you're interested in developing a technique that moves at nearly the speed of instinct by making use of the principles of

MUSCLE MEMORY.

Let me explain:

Muscle memory is a catch-phrase which refers to the brain's ability to learn a complex task so that it can be performed automatically, that is without devoting conscious thought to the process.

Of course, to accomplish this you must first <u>consciously</u> practice the individual parts of the complex task, slowly and perfectly (accurately) since the expression "garbage in-garbage out" applies to this process perfectly.

If at any point during the learning process you reinforce incorrect actions, those inaccuracies become part of the complex task and you will fail to accomplish your goal.

On the other hand, if you are precise and careful to be accurate and slow in learning the components of the complex task, you will eventually be able to increase both your accuracy and speed in the performance of the complete task.

Precision is a learned skill. The process begins with sensory input, either visual (such as notes on the page) or auditory (such as a melodic line heard). At first, we must think through what the notes are: what is the note's name, fingering, sound, value, dynamic, etc? Then we consciously apply the answers to those questions to play the note.

Over time the process becomes automatic: we sight read accurately, producing not only the proper notes, with the proper values, intonation, rhythmic value and dynamics, but also the proper phrasing. With experienced jazz musicians simply hearing a "lick" is sufficient for them to reproduce it.

In the science of kinesthetics, this is called "kinesthetic memory" or "sensory-motor learning". In other words:

Input Sensation / Output Action/Reaction

You view the note, and your body plays the note, without your conscious thought process needing to be applied.

Sound like science fiction? It's not, though!

Suppose you have a lick in a piece of music that has been giving you some trouble. The traditional approach would be to play it, perhaps over and over, without giving a lot of thought to the process.
Here's the muscle memory approach:

> Break the section into 2 or 3 note sequences.
>
> Play the first sequence, to the first note of the second sequence, but do so VERY slowly, with very precise movements of your fingers on the valves and your lip actions.
>
> Repeat the sequence, 8-12 times in a row, without counting times when you make a mistake.
>
> Then repeat the process for the next sequence of notes.

Then combine those first two sequences and follow the precision and repetition procedure.

Only increase the speed, by a maximum of 3 or 4 clicks on the metronome, when you are able to do all 12 repetitions without error.

Remember that it takes time to establish a good habit. The same can be said of making use of muscle memory.

Be patient. After several days of repetition, with small increases in metronome speed, you will be ready to try the sequence at performance tempo.

Be prepared to be amazed at the results!

SWIMMING THROUGH TECHNIQUE

You may have been taught (as I was) to "bang" the trumpet valves down full-force. The trouble is, that approach leads more often to repetitive stress injury, tendonitis, and even mis-aligned valves (on occasion) than it does to technical facility.

So what's a trumpeter to do?

Well, in the first place, if you have hard or stiff springs in your valves you might want to try lighter action springs.

You might also like to try a technique that I've found helpful both for myself and my students. I call it "swimming through technical studies," but don't worry: I won't ask you to play your trumpet under water!

The premise is simple. Try the following activities to acclimate yourself to the process:

> First, move your fingers quickly through the air.
>
> Next, fill a basin, tub or sink with warm (not hot) water.
>
> Place your right hand into the water so that it is completely submerged but not touching any surface.
>
> Just allow your hand to float gently in the water.
>
> Now move your fingers as if playing your valves, first slowly, then gradually faster and faster.
>
> You'll notice that there is a smoothness to the action as the water creates a slight drag to the movement of your fingers.

Now let's go back to the horn.

Let's apply the same feeling to the way we PUSH (not bang) the valves on the horn. You may find it easiest to reproduce if you keep your fingers relatively straight and move them from the knuckles at the base of the fingers. Avoid curling the fingers (it introduces tension into the hands).

As you play, try to keep the feeling of moving your fingers (and valves) as smoothly as if they were still under the surface of the water.

It may help to remember the "curve ball" shape of your right hand as we discussed in Chapter 2. The palm of your hand should not touch the leadpipe. The fingers should curve gently (almost staying straight) from the base of the fingers and stay relaxed as possible (never claw-like).

The right thumb should rest gently under the leadpipe, between the first and second valve casings and remain straight or curved as necessary to keep the pads of the fingers (not the tips) on the valve buttons.

WOODSHEDDING APPROACH TO PRACTICING

How do you learn new music or increase your technical ability on continuing repertoire?

One technique, which we'll call "woodshedding," helps to develop muscle memory by systematically dividing and conquering technical passages through repetition.

Am I repeating myself? Good! Because, as my dear friend Hayr Sourp Minassian says "Repetition is the essence of learning. Repeat!"

We'll use Arban's Characteristic Etude number 13 (P. 297 in the Carl Fischer edition of *Arban's Complete Conservatory Method*) to demonstrate the process.

Play the first chromatic triplet to the first note of the second triplet, slowly and precisely. (G-F#-G-A) Repeat this sequence, slowly, 8-12 times.

Now play the second triplet to the first note of the third triplet, again very slowly and precisely. (A-G-F#-G) Again, repeat this series of notes 8-12 times, very slowly, and don't count a repetition if you make a mistake.

Next, combine the first two triplets and play to the first note of the third triplet.

(G-F#-G A-G-F# G)

Play this combined series for the 8 to 12 repetitions. Begin to increase the speed slowly and precisely (only 3-4 clicks on the metronome!).

Because the third and fourth triplets echo the first and second, you can now add the four triplets together to the first note of the fifth triplet.

(G-F#-G A-G-F# G-F#-G A-G-F# G)

Repeat this sequence 8 to 12 times in succession, again maintaining the accuracy and slow tempo.

By following this process throughout the entire piece, you will establish muscle memory and eventually be able to play the piece seemingly faster than conscious thought, without cramping your hand. (For a joyful experience of this piece, listen to the recording of the Philip Jones Brass Ensemble playing it in transcription for solo trumpet with brass quartet: delightful!)

This woodshedding technique, though it takes time to accomplish, provides security and speed to your fingering technique and can also be used to develop tonguing facility.

Be sure to keep your hands and fingers as relaxed as possible throughout the process. Visualize your fingers moving swiftly and smoothly—under water- and you'll soon be "swimming" through all manner of technical work!

CHAPTER 13

EXTREME TECHNIQUES

Save it 'til You Need It!

Many trumpet players make use of extreme techniques every day. For example: have you seen a trumpet player clench his face to hit a high note? Or how about squeezing the valve casing until her knuckles turned white?

Less obvious, of course, are those extreme techniques which pass for every day approaches to playing. These are the most insidiously dangerous things you can do if you want to maintain, preserve, or develop your chops. Used on an occasional basis, like the poisonous jelly fish prized by Sushi eaters, they may help you get through a particularly tiring day or a gig that runs far into overtime.

Used on a daily basis, however, they can cause Berlin Walls of obstacles to your growth and can even stop you from playing completely.

That caveat noted, let's look at some of the EXTREME techniques that our taskmistress sometimes requires of us:

I. ***"My chops are completely DEAD, and I've got one more short set to go on this killer gig! What can I do to keep going?"***

Okay, the first thing you SHOULD have done was prepare for the gig by practicing every day after doing the *Daily Diagnostic CHOPCHECK*^{TM}! But perhaps you are a weekend warrior who has limited practice time during the week.

But here you are, ON the gig, when your chops start to cave. You could pass off the lead charts to another of the trumpeters (oh, you're the *only* trumpeter?!!?)

> **NOTE BENE**: Do NOT use this technique more than once, as it could lead to nerve damage if abused! If you are under the age of 21, DO NOT USE THIS TECHNIQUE AT ALL!!!!

Here is a last ditch technique that will offer you limited relief:

1. Open your mouth very wide.
2. Insert a fingertip into the very back of your mouth so that it meets the soft tissue between the jaws at the side of your mouth.
3. Press HARD until you feel the muscles at the front of your mouth relax (you may get a tingling feeling also).

This will grant you 15-20 minute more of playing time in a pinch, but will REQUIRE taking several days off to rest (using ice and NO playing!) afterward.

II. Sliding the mouthpiece down, into the edge of the red of the upper lip.

Be VERY wary of using this technique. Yes, it will get you a bit more range in a pinch, but relying on it on a regular basis <u>will</u> cause injury to the lip membrane, resulting in swelling, bruising and possible cyst development.

III. Using the tip of the tongue, (ala Callet TCE) to support the lips

This can be very useful when your chops are very fatigued. Simply place the tip of the tongue against the inside of the lips where the top lip meets the bottom lip.

I encourage you to obtain Jerry Callet's book: "Trumpet Secrets-Secrets of the Tongue Controlled Embouchure" for further information.

IV. Using the "eee" syllable

This will provide you with a very "bright" sound that will project easily, but you run the risk of pressurized air leaking through the soft palette and rushing up into the nasal sinuses, causing headaches and black-outs. Beware! It would be far better to use a rolling inward of the lips (make the red disappear).

V. Using an extreme pivot

Again, fatigue may drive you to use a much more drastic pivot than usual. Be careful of this, because it, too, can cause bruising of lip tissues because the lips are required to accept more pressure than they normally do.

VI. Puffing the cheeks

This is not as drastic a tactic as it might first appear to be. Many jazz trumpeters will use puffing of one or both cheeks to achieve a foggy nature to their tone for specific ballads. (Think of Chet Baker). Again, though, use it sparingly, for special effect, rather than all the time.

VII. Switching to a larger mouthpiece than you would normally use

This can be used for swollen chops (though it would be better to take a few days off instead!). It can also be used to recover from injury, by forcing you to use larger muscle groups. Again, be very careful about this!

VIII. Switching the placement of your Chopset (Ignoring your natural anchor spot)

Save this for injury recovery, or use with a cornetto (zink) mouthpiece; this is quite different from a regular mouthpiece and you may find it more responsive with the mouthpiece placed in the corner of your lips. Be aware, though, that your response, flexibility and tone color will suffer from the change.

As in so many areas in life: moderation is the better part of valor. Don't use extreme techniques if you can avoid them! If you must use them, use them for very limited periods of time.

CHAPTER 14

Fix-Its
Recovering from Fatigue or Injury

Well, now you've done it! You've over-played, under-prepared, and hurt yourself.

Did you really think you needed to try and overblow the lead guitarist on that rock gig?

It's time to practice healing yourself. The first step is an honest evaluation of the damage.

If all you've done is exhaust your chops, you'll probably be fine after 2-3 days of rest—OFF HORN!

That's right, I said "Off Horn!" No practicing, no picking up the horn just to check and see if you're better. Serious down time, without playing, for several days is really the best approach to overuse of the chops.

It will also help to "ice" the lips. I like to use soft-serve ice cream for this: the texture is soothing; the temperature is not quite as drastic as straight ice would be, and it tastes good!

Use your lips to "bite" at the ice cream, and swirl it around inside your lips and your mouth before swallowing.

ELDERLY TRUMPETERS

For trumpeters over the age of 70 the biggest issue may be that of increased time frames, both for development of musculature and for healing in case of injury.

Musically, older players are often far ahead of youngsters with interpretation, but may need to be more vigilant about marking their music, making sure that they have special glasses for reading music (an intermediate distance, not like driving or reading glasses), and may need to ask for adaptive seating in ensembles (to better see the conductor).

I've known many trumpeters who continued to perform well into their nineties! And perform well they did!

LIP SWELLING

A few pointers about lip swelling, which can be caused by many factors, but will be alleviated by doing the following:

1. Do gentle horseflaps (slow, floppy lip buzzing, away from the mpc/horn)

2. Do double-low pedal tones for 3-5 minutes 3-4 times per day (these begin at the C two octaves below middle C/first line below the staff, and will also help you with range, airflow and endurance.)

3. Ice the lips, 20 minutes on, 20 minutes off.

4. Don't play on severely swollen lips: they'll bruise more easily and deep bruising can take a lot longer to heal than you might think.

5. Be careful after dental work: Novocain often causes a lot of swelling in lip and gum tissues, and can be especially irritating when it's injected deep into tissues (to affect nerves). Give it time to wear off.

Personally, I find that I can still feel (or rather, NOT feel) the effects of short-acting Novocain for several days after a dental procedure.

BE CAREFUL TO AVOID PLAYING TOO LOUDLY!!

Playing too loudly, besides causing the lips to swell, can also cause *pressure blisters* which can lead to the formation of scar tissue and even cysts (if you are prone to developing them).

STAY WELL-HYDRATED!

Drink ample water while playing. Let me repeat that:

DRINK A LOT OF WATER BEFORE, DURING, AND AFTER PLAYING!!!!!

> **N.B**. If you have kidney disease, be sure to consult with your doctor before making any changes.

The reason for this is simple. Our bodies are made up of high percentages of water, and when we are dehydrated (don't have enough fluid in our systems), the body resorts to tactics to preserve tissues by using lymph fluid (swelling) to make up for the missing water in the cells (simplified explanation, so don't go crazy trying to complicate it, folks).

The ONLY way to prevent this is by drinking adequate water.

Water refreshes you, keeps your mouth and lips moist, keeps your throat and lungs from drying out, etc.

A good benchmark is to drink 4-8 oz. of water (sipping periodically) during every 45 minutes of playing. And, just for good measure (no pun intended), drink 4-8 oz. before you start to play, and another 4-8 oz when you are done.

Yes, you will need to visit the restroom more often. But it's worth it to avoid the swelling problem.

6. Cut excess sodium from your diet. This means limiting carbonated beverages, pizza, Chinese food (unless it's without MSG), packaged prepared foods (modified food starch), pretzels (unless unsalted) or popcorn (unless unsalted and unbuttered), etc. By the way, you might just improve your health along the way.

7. Avoid alcohol, coffee and any other caffeinated beverages (that includes chocolate, tea, and CHAI tea), as they cause your body to lose fluids faster. In fact, if you drink one 6 oz cup of coffee (or one 6 oz. can of soda) you need to drink 12 oz of water to replace the water lost and get back the benefit of the 6 oz of WATER you should have drunk in the first place!) Caffeine can also exacerbate performance anxiety/nerves.

8. Do not use camphor or menthol on your lips. Desert Essence puts out a product called *Lip Rescue* which contains tea tree oil, as well as non-toxic emollients (no lanolin), which works very nicely to heal sore lips of every sort, including chapped lips.

9. Avoid sun on your lips. This may seem obvious, but you'd be surprised how many people go out in the sun without sunscreen on their lips (Zinc Oxide ointment is the best, comes in different colors for fun, is a total block), and wind up with sun blisters, which act like cold sores.

10. Adhere to a regular schedule of playing EVERY day. This accommodates your lip tissues to the stress of vibration and they will toughen up. DON't overdo, however. Far better to do several 5-10 minute sessions spread out, than one 45-60 minute session all at once, particularly if you're a CP (comeback player).

11. Be careful of your aftershave lotion (try to avoid getting it onto your lips). Same goes for makeup, ladies: if your makeup contains alpha hydroxy it will dry out your lips and cause them to peal off the top layer just like it does to your skin (how did you THINK it made the wrinkles appear to disappear!)

12. Avoid hot foods and beverages, which may burn your lips on the way in. Often when we burn our tongue we forget that the lips have also been burned. (Especially beware of fast food hot coffee, which is frequently astronomically hot!)

13. In the same vein, avoid excessively spicy foods (for the same reason as in number 12!)

14. Consider changing to a gold-plated mouthpiece, or have your mouthpiece refinished (sometimes microscopic pits in the mpc rim may harbor bacteria or repeatedly injure your lips at contact).

15. Be sure that you are not rolling your lips inward, covering over the edges of the teeth (like you're pretending you have no teeth). This can traumatize the delicate lip membrane.

16. Take a mild anti-inflammatory such as aspirin or Tylenol (acetaminophen) before playing (afterwards won't help as much). Drink plenty of WATER with it (16 oz of water is good, drink 4-8 oz beforehand, swallow the pill with another 4 oz, then finish the water).

17. This is a no-brainer, but I have to say it anyway: Avoid heavy pressure kissing. Teach your wife, husband, boyfriend, girlfriend to respect your chops. And don't kiss ANYone on the lips who has any type of sore there. It isn't worth the risk of catching a cold sore (if you're susceptible).

18. Also,(this I learned from Leon Merian many years ago <THANK-YOU, TMBTH!>), before playing on your mouthpiece, rub it on the side of your neck or your cheek to make sure the pH balance is correct for your skin. This will avoid getting any comedos on your lips (vernacular word is pimples).

19. It goes without saying that you should not be applying excess mouthpiece pressure to your lips. The only pressure you need is just enough to seal the mpc against the lips, which are sealed against each other. And you are playing with wet lips, AREN'T YOU?!!?

20. Finally, be sure that you have the mouthpiece placed correctly. In my experience as a teacher (35 + years, now), I've found that students with thick lips will sometimes place the mpc down, into the red (membrane) of the lips.

This tissue is very FRAGILE and can't handle that sort of stress. It's important to place the inner, upper edge of the rim just above the ridge where the red (membrane) meets the white/brown (muscle) of the upper lip, at a minimum (some players place it even higher). If you are cutting off the red of the lip it can't vibrate properly and you will have problems with swelling, range, endurance and tone quality.

The following are more serious issues, with more serious consequences for your playing and more need for professional treatment.

ACNE/ROSACEA

This is a sensitive issue for those who suffer from it. Best advice is to maintain absolutely obsessive cleanliness (change your razor blade on a daily basis, avoid touching the affected areas, cleanse according to your health care professional's advice) and be religious about watching your intake of food.

Zinc, in ointment or oral supplement, may be beneficial. Ask your health care professional if it is appropriate for you. Do be <u>very</u> careful about using medicines such as Accutane, which can dry your skin so severely that your lips will develop deep, painful cracks.

If you do develop serious cracking of the lips, be careful about using over the counter medicines to treat them (such as Triple Antibiotic Ointment), since certain medications could make the cracks worse.

Best advice: consult a dermatologist, but be sure to discuss with them the fact that you are a trumpet player.

DENTAL ISSUES

This can be a painful subject for trumpet players. Bottom line: take care of your teeth and gums and you're less likely to require the most drastic measures in dental intervention.

For what it's worth, I don't recommend altering your natural teeth alignment or shape, especially if you've been playing on them for a number of years. The reason for this is that your lips have become accustomed to the feeling of your teeth and changes will require time to adapt to the sensation and to recreate the muscle memory of fine-motor control of your chops.

To avoid a worst case scenario, such as tooth damage from an accident, DO ask your primary dentist to make a mold of your teeth for future reference. Failing to do so may make it difficult (or impossible) to replicate your original tooth structure in the event of an emergency.

If you must have dental work done, ask the dentist what other options there are besides Novocain. Novocain causes swelling besides numbness, and both can take quite a bit of time to wear off. Anyone who's bitten the inside of their cheek or lip while under the influence of Novocain can relate to this.

There is also a short-acting Novocain that will stop the discomfort during dental work but be less likely to last too long. (For some it wears off in about an hour, but I find I can still feel the effects for several days.)

DIABETES

A number of my adult students have issues with diabetes, the most frustrating of which is that it takes them much longer to recover from fatigue or injury than it did before their diabetes became acute.

If you are a diabetic trumpeter it should go without saying that you must be vigilant about checking your blood sugar on a daily basis. You must also be very careful about your diet and medications.

You may need to allot extra time between rehearsals and performances, and it is likely that you might need to take some time off from playing to recuperate after a strenuous performance.

But the good news is that with a well-managed diet, exercise and medication program, you will probably have better strength and endurance than you might have had before your condition was diagnosed.

Please be sure to stay in contact with your health care professional, and be extra careful about avoiding triggers to your condition.

BRACES

If you absolutely MUST have orthodontia, I encourage you to investigate *"Invisalign."* This is a new type of orthodontia that does not require wires between the front of the teeth and the lips. I understand that it is not appropriate for every orthodontic need, but for those who are eligible it can save a great deal of discomfort.

CAVEAT EMPTOR (Buyer beware!): Be aware that the profit margin for dentists is not as high with *Invisalign*, so some may discourage its use even when appropriate. Be a smart shopper and investigate your options thoroughly.

If, however, you do have the traditional wire type of braces, you may find some relief by using the *Morgan Bumper*, which is a device that covers over the wires with a channeled tube of PVC. Type the following link into your browser on your computer for more detailed information: **(https://www.morganbumper.com/index1.html)**

ASTHMA/EMPHYSEMA/COPD

If you have pulmonary disease, you have my sympathies, but please don't take it as a sentence dooming you to giving up playing your horn.

My very first student, in 1970, was a young boy with asthma. His pediatrician had recommended playing the trumpet as a way to cope with his asthma. The idea was that playing the trumpet would encourage deeper breathing, supported by back and abdominal muscles that would help to better expel the air from his lungs. (In asthma, muscles surrounding the branches of the lungs spasm shut causing the typical "wheezing" sound of asthma).

Much later, due to an industrial accident, I, too, developed severe asthma. When my asthma is acute I struggle with lower register playing, but upper register tends to be okay. (Though I admit I sometimes have to adapt my phrasing to account for lowered capacity.)

Using lots of water (particularly cold and/or ice water) seems to help, as does avoiding irritants in the air. (I use the recirculation knob in my car a lot!)

Avoid situations that would require you to be exposed to exhaust fumes or cigarette smoke. Even smoke from cooking can be an issue: use an exhaust fan whenever possible.

Hardware stores, such as Ace, True Value, or Home Depot carry air purifiers that help to cleanse the air in your home during those months when air conditioners are not an option.

Be vigilant about avoiding mold growth in kitchens, bathrooms and basements, too.

Ask your doctor if long-acting bronchodilators may be appropriate for you. There are many possibilities, and if you are using your *Peak Flow Meter* on a daily basis, (as you should!) you should be able to manage your symptoms well enough to keep playing.

If you are treated with prednisone or other steroids, be aware that it may cause swelling of the lips that will impede your ability to seal the lips well until the swelling subsides (usually several weeks to several months after stopping the use of steroids).

In addition, some oral medications may make it difficult to use the small motor muscles of the embouchure, particularly those that are designed to relax the muscles of the bronchi.

SMOKING

If you are a smoker, try using the patch to quit. (Talk to your primary care physician!) There are generic brands now as well as the original *Nicoderm*. There is also now a prescription pill, called CHANTIX, which has helped some of my students in quitting. I'm told that if you stop smoking you can expect your lungs to return to near normal after 6 months to a year without exposure to smoke.

I also sympathize that smoking is one of the most difficult addictions to break, but it's NOT impossible!

You can do this! Talk to your health care professional. Take up chewing gum, use toothpicks, get a set of *Chopsticks* lip exercisers (and use them!).

You can find substitutes for your oral stimulation impulses.

Your lungs will thank you, and so will your family members and colleagues!

RECOVERING FROM SERIOUS ILLNESS

Be aware that recovery from illness takes time. Trumpet playing is strenuous, in a cardio-vascular context, so don't be surprised if it takes you several months to feel like you normally do when playing.

When you do start to play again, take it slowly: work on Clarke Technical Studies, Graves' Fundamental Flexibilities, and intermediate level etudes by Sigmund Hering, Ernest Williams, Leonard Smith, and Egil Smedvig (Rolf's Dad). The idea is to get your lips vibrating and your air flowing, without straining.

STREP THROAT

Don't play with a severe sore throat or you risk blowing bacteria up, through the Eustachian tubes, into the inner ear.

Gargle with warm, salt water. Finish the complete course of antibiotics prescribed by your physician (ALWAYS finish antibiotics, unless you have an allergic reaction to them. Don't discontinue the antibiotics when you feel better because if you do you are contributing to the bacteria's being resistant to that particular antibiotic. This is how "super bugs" are born!)

SINUS ISSUES

Flushing with salt water solutions can help, as can learning to blow your nose properly (so that you're not affecting your eardrums!).

If you absolutely MUST play with a head cold, talk to your doctor or pharmacist about possible medications. Often topical medications, such as nose sprays can be used on a short term basis.

Beware of using them for extended periods of time, however, since you can develop a dependency on them (and get a rebound effect that will block your sinuses even worse!)

COLD SORES

There are many newer options for treating cold sores. Ask your doctor or pharmacist about them.

Boil your mouthpiece and spray Lysol into your mouthpiece case and your trumpet case where it touches the mouthpiece and allow it to dry (preferably in the sun).

Do not share mouthpieces or lip balm if you are prone to cold sores.

CYSTS

I know of an accomplished trumpet player who developed a cyst on the upper lip, right at the anchor spot, from playing with too much pressure for an extended period of time (as lead trumpet for a traveling show).

This trumpeter went to the doctor, first a general practitioner, then a dermatologist, to learn about options for treatment.

The dermatologist described a cystectomy: opening the tissue, excising the cyst, cleaning and packing the area, possibly closing with a stitch or two, cleansing regularly and treating with antibiotics.

The trumpeter went home to think about the procedure, and then decided to do something VERY foolish:

This trumpeter performed the cystectomy on himself.

I am NOT endorsing this, merely describing the sort of extremes to which some of us will resort when faced with a chop emergency.

As it turns out, this particular case had a happy ending: the wound healed, there is a very tiny scar (barely even visible), and there was no adverse affect to the trumpeter's embouchure.

The result, however, could have been drastically different: the blade could have slipped, cutting the lip too deeply; infection could have set in, nerves might have been affected, etc.

When faced with a chop issue, be sure to consult with medical/dental professionals. You can get second or third opinions, and make sure that you have someone who understands your needs as a trumpeter. Don't make the mistake of thinking you can do it all yourself!

SPLIT LIPS

In general, these can be healed by using "Tea tree oil" or similar natural applications. Many players find that *"Chop Saver"* lip salve is beneficial. It is an herbal blend, with vitamin E and other emollients, that soothes the lips as they heal. It also includes willow tree bark, a natural anti-inflammatory.

An old-timer's remedy for split lips is to apply *Campho-Phenique* liquid to the lips. This hurts to apply, but it will close a split almost immediately and enable you to play out the rest of a gig.

The best way to avoid split lips is the same way to avoid chapped lips: avoid going outside in cold, dry weather with wet lips. Coat your lips with a petroleum type ointment to protect them from the osmotic nature of moisture. Water travels from the area of greatest concentration (aka your lips) to the area of least concentration (the dry air). If your lips do not become seriously dried out and chapped, they are less likely to split open.

CANKER SORES

Make sure that you eat a well-balanced diet, and perhaps supplement with vitamins (especially vitamin C, the B vitamins, and zinc, which helps with the healing process).

Check with your physician or pharmacist about your particular needs in this area. For most people, a multi-vitamin is a good idea. However, there are some medications and conditions for which you must be very careful about supplements. When in doubt, check it out with your doctor!

If the canker is from inadvertently biting the inside of your lip or cheek, you may get good results from "Gly-Oxide" (commercial name for "carbamide peroxide") which contains glycerin and a less irritating form of peroxide. Don't use straight peroxide, though, because it can burn the sensitive mucous membranes inside your mouth.

Using 8 to 10 drops of Gly-Oxide and swishing for 2-3 minutes, plus repeating this process several times a day for 3 to 4 days should clear up the canker sore. I learned this from my childhood dentist, Dr. Herman Weisler, who had been my father's colonel in the Army Medical Corps, and it works well.

PULLED MUSCLES IN THE FACE

This needs to be handled in much the same way you'd handle a pulled muscle elsewhere in your body: use ice (20 minutes on, 20 minutes off) for the first 24 hours, then alternate heat and ice.

You may also wish to take an anti-inflammatory such as Tylenol (acetaminophen), or Alleve (naproxen sodium). Talk to your doctor or pharmacist about your prescription medications before supplementing them with anything else.

When you return to playing after this injury, begin very slowly and gently. Be certain to make use of your natural Anchor Spot^{TM} and avoid loud dynamics.

TOOTH THROUGH THE LIP

This is one of those nightmare situations that, thankfully, doesn't occur that often. When it does, it can be devastating. I have had young students who bit through their lip as a result of a fall, and older colleagues who suffered from a car accident (or bicycle accident).

While it doesn't always require surgery, it's a good idea to be checked out by a facial surgeon just to be sure that no musculature is involved. Flesh wounds will often heal with (or even without) a simple stitch or two. Muscular wounds require more extensive surgical attention and much more time off-horn.

TORN FACIAL MUSCLE

This is really the worst-case scenario. It usually occurs because a player becomes very fatigued and starts to over-blow his chops.

Usually there is a sudden, sharp pain followed by an inability to close and seal the lips. Sometimes holding the cheek that has ruptured will enable brief episodes of playing, but in the long run the only recourse is to undergo reconstructive surgery.

FACING ORAL OR MAXILLO FACIAL SURGERY

Facial surgery need not be a death knell for a trumpet player. Being honest with your surgeon and seeking second (or third, or fourth) opinions can help you locate a surgeon who will cause you the least amount of damage to facial nerves.

When I underwent surgery to remove a tumor from my neck I searched the world over to find a surgeon who would perform the least invasive procedure possible. (Thank-you to Ellis Workman, for sage advice and referrals!)

The first surgeons I consulted explained that they would have to cut open the entire front of my neck, severing facial nerves in the process (and that I'd be lucky to be alive and shouldn't worry about trumpet playing!).

I finally found an excellent surgeon, Dr. Richard Fabian, at Mass Eye and Ear Infirmary, right here in Boston, MA. Dr. Fabian was able to excise the tumor and the pertinent lymph glands without injuring the facial nerves (other than some very minor nerves under the base of my chin). Though he did have to remove the center of the hyoid bone, to which the growth was attached, he was able to do so with a relatively small incision.

I probably suffered a bit more discomfort in the short term as a result of his having to tug and pull to remove the tumor, but it was well worth it to me not to lose my ability to play.
In fact, I was able to buzz my lips in the recovery room!
I hope that you never have to suffer injury to your chops, but if you do, I encourage you to seek the best possible medical advice.

May God grant you swift and complete healing!

CHAPTER 15

Making Lasting Changes

It's all well and good to talk about changing bad habits for good ones, but how do you ensure that the new habits continue?

First, remember that all of us change on a daily basis, in many different ways.

However, it can be a daunting proposal to abandon habits you've practiced for 10, 20, 30 years or even for most of your life!

But it is NOT impossible.

Let me encourage you to take this process one step at a time. Perhaps your first project will be that of relaxing your hands, or your general posture. A next step might be playing with wetter chops, or more open teeth, or locating and making use of your anchor spot.

It is important to remember that early stage accuracy is crucial to establishing good performance habits. Only perfection in practice will lead to perfection in performance, and we develop increasing accuracy through repetition of precise movements.

We must also remember that change is a gradual process, and that we must not only establish the need for a change and the motivation (why do we want to change), but also learn the changed actions and responses.

It is imperative to reinforce new habits on a <u>daily</u> basis.

The great contemporary apologist, Og Mandino, wrote a book entitled "The Greatest Salesman in the World". In this book he uses a parable to present a series of scrolls, which help to establish good habits. I encourage you to get this book and read it. Whether you choose to follow the prescribed daily reading schedule (or not) I leave up to you, but even if you only read the book once it will offer you some good ideas about changing habits.

One of the principles presented in this book is that it takes fourteen (14) days to establish a new habit. Two weeks of daily reinforcement will establish a good habit (or a bad one!).

Is it worth it to you to practice newer, healthier habits in trumpet playing for two weeks?

You need to be consistent and faithful in <u>daily</u> practice in order to truly establish these new habits. You don't need to play 3 or 4 hours at a time in order to do so. Two or three 30 minute sessions every day will more than establish your new approach. And be sure to do many repetitions of each exercise you intend to master. After all: "Repetition is the Essence of Learning!"

Over the course of two or three months, you'll see drastic changes in your playing that you might not have dreamed possible.

By the time you've been playing with your new habits for 6 months to a year, your friends, section mates, families and colleagues will be delighted at your progress.

And what about you, yourself?

Well, frankly, one of the first things that you must do if you are to make a lasting change is to commit to the process. If you think that you are not capable of making the change, or you tell yourself "it's going to be hard to change," you're right, it <u>will</u> be hard!

But, if you tell yourself that you "CAN do this!" you will do it!

There is an interesting processing that occurs between the conscious, thinking mind and the subconscious, instinctive mind. I call it:

WHAT YOUR MOUTH SAYS YOUR MIND BELIEVES!

Strangely enough, when you say positive things about yourself (especially out loud, but even to yourself), you begin to believe them!

You can experience this by trying something very simple:

Tell yourself (out loud) "It's getting warmer in this room."

Repeat the statement several times as you do something else. After a while, you'll find yourself needing to remove your jacket or sweater, or wanting to open a window!

You can also do this by "finding your center" through a meditation technique such as Tai Chi.

Follow the following process:

1. Stand or sit in a relaxed fashion.
2. Allow your hands to float by your side.
3. Now, as you slowly breathe deeply in, through your nose, bring your hands gradually up to the top of your head.
4. As you reach full capacity, turn your hands around and "push" against the air as you lower your hands while breathing slowly out through your mouth (purse your lips slightly and put some "spin" on the air).
5. Repeat this process seven times in succession.
6. Now bring your hands to the center of your body, just in front of your belly-button or navel.
7. Cup your hands against each other as if you were holding a softball between them (palms facing each other).
8. Concentrate (always breathing deeply and calmly: in through your nose and out through pursed lips) until you can feel heat radiating between your palms.
9. Once you can feel the heat, gradually draw your hands apart, but try to maintain the sensation of feeling heat moving between them.

With practice you'll find that you can bring your hands completely apart, to the width of your shoulders or greater and *still feel the heat*! You might even feel your hands begin to sweat.

You can also concentrate and teach yourself to make your hands feel cool or cold.

How is this possible?

This is a prime example of "mind over matter." You have the innate ability to control your body's reaction to stimuli.

This is the principle behind the "fire-walkers" who walk barefoot over hot coals. By controlling the mind, you control the body.

Of course, this takes time and conditioning both your body and your mind, but it is completely possible to accomplish.

Persons who've survived abuse often speak of being "outside myself" and being "an observer." These are protective mechanisms that serve to enhance survival.

Now, I'm not suggesting you subject yourself to abuse of ANY type! Quite the contrary.

But I <u>am</u> encouraging you to explore mind over body concepts to assist you in your journey as a trumpeter.

As a cartoon figure used to shout "You have the POWER!"

Don't be afraid to use it!

CHAPTER 16

Painting a Personal Style
The Palette Approach to Trumpet Playing

For many years, I've used the concept with more advanced students of developing their personal palette of trumpet skills, both physical and interpretative.

I find the concept useful because, like artists who use paint, we as trumpet artists begin to play with just a few options and gradually develop more and more as we mature.

My personal approach may be likened to that of a teacher of painting. (Note that I do frequent personal demonstrations throughout the process.)

Let me explain:

When a person teaches another to paint, they begin with absolute basics, which may seem to have little or nothing to do with the final product, for example: figure studies, sculpting, drawing with pencil or chalk, mixing colors. And all this is covered before the student is even allowed to pick up a paintbrush (and then, that is often only to learn how to CLEAN the brush, not to use it).

A gradual process is followed in which the student develops a personal palette of colors, as well as a personal palette (if you will) of techniques which will enable the highest degrees of self-expressive creation in the future.

Often hours will be spent on a single brush stroke, perfecting the angle, the beginning, and the completion of the stroke. Then the same technique will be repeated, this time adding layers of paint to the brush to produce graduated color for, say, a leaf or the curve of a blossom.

When we begin to play the trumpet, we focus on the purely physical aspects of playing to establish a good foundation for the future. This makes sense, since we don't build a house from the roof downward, but from the foundation upward.

For example: a young player is usually content just to play the correct notes to a piece. A slightly more mature player pays close attention to articulations and dynamics. An artist knows that there are internal dynamics and secondary articulations that can be applied to gain subtle effects, which less experienced players often don't recognize, except to understand that, for some reason, the playing of a particular player moves them more deeply than most.

How do you develop a personal palette? Through practice, through listening, through performing a wide variety of styles.

When I was an undergraduate I never turned down ANY opportunity to perform, including with experimental, black box theater productions, a rock-a-billy band that played for dance class, wind ensemble, symphony and chamber orchestra, marching and jazz bands, brass quintet, as well as vocal classes (accompanying basses, baritones and sopranos on Bach, Handel, Purcell, Scarlatti, etc), and the Collegium Musicum (in which I learned to play Renaissance instruments.

This granted a subtlety of articulation that lends itself beautifully to the trumpet and piccolo trumpet, as well as interpretative dynamics that lend themselves well to all periods of music).

Each unique experience lent me the opportunity to expand my personal palette. The Stravinsky Octet taught me about adjusting my pitch to play with the bassoon in the extreme upper register (which is much harder to adjust than is the trumpet's pitch). Working with vocalists, from youngsters to seasoned professionals, taught me to experiment with vibrato widths and speeds to alter timbre. (Nothing is as exhilarating for a soprano as to have a trumpeter who not only matches pitch, but also vibrato with her).

Playing in experimental theater productions taught me much about aleatoric music, and alternative techniques, as well as challenging me to produce a wide variety of timbres.

And those are just a few of many, many examples I could cite.

How many different attacks can you produce with a single tongue? How do you alter the tongue stroke to produce a different effect? Try to changing the shape of the tip of your tongue while single tonguing as well as changing the location where that tip strikes. Record yourself to hear what happens.

Of course, you should also practice so that YOU are in control of whether the pitch and timbre change with attacks or not.

Practice Arban's and Clarke's exercises with every imaginable variation of articulation: legato, marcato, slurred, tongued, double tongued, triple tongued, fanfare tongued, syncopated, etc.

Experiment with altering your airspeed and the amount of air you use for a particular note or dynamic level.

Experiment with various types of vibrato:

1. Lip vibrato (varying pitch via compression and release of lip muscles, though not enough to change overtones, unless for a wide jazz shake)

2. Jaw vibrato (using an upward and downward, or less often a side to side motion of the jaw, as in "ah-yah-yah")

3. Hand vibrato (extremely delicate effect, created by moving fingers back and forth on valve caps)

4. Wrist vibrato (as in hand vibrato, but moving from the wrist, which makes for a slightly more dramatic effect)

5. Arm vibrato (as in wrist vibrato, but moving from the elbow)

6. Diaphragm vibrato (as in "huh-huh-huh" alteration of the airstream from the abdomen-- perhaps the most difficult)

7. Throat vibrato (not recommended/hazardous for some)

Any or all of these techniques can be developed with practice, and should only be used as ornaments, not justifications of sound ("the icing, not the cake.")

It is in repetitive practicing that we develop the palette of muscle memory that enables us to perform without consciously considering the details while in performance.

MARK your music, paying special attention to internal dynamics (gentler dynamics that occur within a phrase), alternate fingerings, specific articulations.

Listen to ALL types of music (and that includes woodwinds, especially classical ones). Listen to articulations, phrasing, and releases.

One of the most revelatory experiences you can have is to practice flowing arpeggios with a really fine clarinetist (try to emulate the smoothness of the flow between notes that is generated by the clarinetist!)

Do you pay attention to the releases of notes or just the attacks? Great musicians manage to be in control of both.

If your attacks are wonderful but your releases are haphazard, your performance will sound unfinished.

Practice breath releases of various sorts as well as tongue releases. Taper notes gently sometimes, even if the written dynamics don't seem to indicate it. Seldom do notes require abrupt, tongued releases. Even staccato and marcato notes will sound cleaner using a breath release rather than a tongued release, particularly if the notes are in a series rather than singular.

Remember, what's written on the page is not music, only rough shorthand to help the performer reproduce what the composer intended. Sheet music only becomes MUSIC when it is interpreted, performed and perceived by an audience.

Practice in both detail and performance modes. One in every three practice sessions should be a "mock" performance in which you emulate your best possible performance (then carry that with you into actual performance).

Subtlety is a key that is all too often forgotten by trumpeters who think only of power and projection. Whisper with your trumpet, or you'll never play the end of the Haydn second movement properly, or the solo in the Gershwin Piano Concerto. You'll have plenty of opportunities to shout through the horn, you know.

Make your pianissimos as intense as a double forte. Can you? Work on it (hint: it's in the air support!)

Make your fortissimos as rounded as a fluegelhorn. Can you? Work on it (hint: it's in the shape of the aperture).

Learn to roll your lips outward and inward to control pitch, projection and timbre.

Communicate with your audience. There is nothing worse than a self-centered performer. I once saw an exquisite performance ruined by a performer finishing a long decrescendo at the end of a piece who abruptly put her instrument down and looked up at the audience as if to say "There! I'm done, now applaud!"

How much better it might have been to maintain the illusion that the note continued, and draw out the suspense so that the audience wasn't quite sure when the piece was over!

We are communicators on our trumpets, but like all communicators we must develop a dynamic vocabulary and style of delivery (and a variety of styles of delivery) to keep our audience listening.

Work every day on your palette. Develop a library of articulations, tone colors, dynamics, and styles.

Your performances will move from "good" to "exquisite!"

CHAPTER 17

Walking the Walk
Practicing What You Teach

For years and years, there has been a dichotomy in approaches to playing the trumpet.

On the one side are those who espouse purely musical principles (such as sound, tone color, interpretation, knowledge of literature, etc.) and avoid the physical aspects of playing as much as possible.

On the other side are those who focus purely on physical aspects (such as embouchure, equipment, breathing, tonguing, etc.) and avoid discussing the esoteric aspects of playing as much as possible.

In the middle are those of us who address both sides, depending upon the current needs of the student(s) at hand.

This is not to say that both sides of the spectrum do not address the needs of their students, just that they may focus too much on one side of the equation, without addressing the other very much.

TEACHING STYLES VS. LEARNING STYLES

Too often teachers, who don't know how to teach, will blame failure on the student instead of the failure of the teacher to identify the best way to teach to the student's particular learning style.

For example, you can't teach a beginner the same way you can a student who's an undergraduate or graduate student in college. CP's (comeback players) have their own unique sets of circumstances, and each must be approached with THEIR needs considered first!

For some, who are AURAL, or ear-centered, learners, it is sufficient to demonstrate so that they may imitate the teacher's sound, attack, style, interpretation, what-have-you.

For others a more clinical approach is necessary, with careful explanations and definitions clarifying the material for the student.

For others, it becomes necessary to cajole the student via experiencing the feeling of producing a particular sound, style or articulation. Once they've internalized the experience they'll be able to reproduce it.

And that, I believe, is the crux of the matter. No teacher, no matter how experienced he or she may be, is able to be with the student for more than a couple of hours per week (and that's if they meet for both lesson and a master class).

In the long run, it is the job of the conscientious teacher to empower the student to teach him/herself, since the student must spend many more hours alone in practicing than they will with anyone else, and must develop a method for providing their own feedback on their progress.

To assume that a teacher's influence is absolute is to pander to that teacher's self-aggrandizement and vanity. And I'd wager that such a teacher would turn away students who'd require more than the usual attention and effort on the part of their teacher, and accept more than an average number of pupils who would have progressed adequately even without ANY outside input at all!

Judge me on my worst students, please, as well as my stars. For the students from whom I (and anyone else) will have learned the most are those who have struggled and persevered, despite the odds being against them.

One more thought. I once taught at a school that had the following quotation prominently displayed on the bulletin board in the teachers' room:

"Teaching is the only profession which affects eternity"

Quite a responsibility in my opinion!

BEGINNING THE PROCESS

When we begin to play the trumpet, we focus on the purely physical aspects of playing to establish a good foundation for the future. This makes sense, since we don't build a house from the roof downward, but from the foundation upward.

The very first step should be learning to take good, solid breaths while using a good, upright but relaxed posture. Once the student has learned to take a good breath (I recommend breathing inward with the mouth in the same shape as if saying the word "HOME." This establishes a habit of dropping the jaw and tongue, filling up with relaxed air, and creating a rounded oral cavity.), I'll move on to getting him/her to wet the lips and close them gently before blowing the wind out with belly support (pulling the belly button in, toward the backbone).

(Note: this is for sheer beginners--I don't always advocate wedge-type breathing for mid-range or lower playing--more about that later.)

This should establish a good "horse-flap" type of buzzing in the lips. (For some students it's also necessary to use the tip of the tongue on the inside of the lips as if spitting out a seed to begin the vibrations, but not all.)

I'll next teach the student to place the tips of the index fingers at the corners of the lips with the fingers straight and tips pointing upward. Then I'll have the student gradually blow harder and compress the lips more strongly against each other as he/she moves the fingertips gently toward the center from both ends (this helps to establish a seal between the lips and to increase the speed of the lip buzz).

(Note: at no time do the fingertips press inward against the lips--they merely rest outside them to keep the awareness of seal there.)

Finally, I'll diagnose the best point-of-compression (Anchor Spot™) for the student before teaching them to apply the mouthpiece to the already established embouchure. It is essential to establish this point-of-compression (Anchor Spot™) because the whole embouchure works best when this is utilized. (It is the point at which the orbicularis oris muscle meets itself somewhere near the midpoint of the upper lip, but varies to some degree among players. It is seldom, if ever, exactly spot-on dead center, by the way.)

I'll have the student hold the mouthpiece shank gently between the thumb and the first two fingers and apply it to wet lips at the anchor spot. We'll adjust the angle and pivot to accommodate the shape of the teeth and type of the jaw. Then we drop the jaw, keeping the upper rim on the upper lip at the anchor spot, breathe "HOME", close the lips and blow into the mpc.

Teeth and jaw shape determine the pivot (up-to-down angle) and angle (side-to-side angle) of the embouchure, not the lips. Thus damage to teeth or jaw usually does not change the anchor spot, though damage to the lip itself (without damage to bone) may change it drastically.

All of this and we haven't even added the trumpet yet!

In fact, if these basics have never been established into muscle memory by the player, even more advanced players may need to return to these exercises in order to continue their advanced development or to break long-standing bad habits.

Of course, during all of this so far, we are continually reinforcing the breathing approach and the relaxed, aligned posture.

Next step is to teach the student to hold the trumpet properly. I NEVER tell the student to "Grip the trumpet firmly like you're shaking a hand" because this immediately leads to tension in the hands and arms.

Instead, I teach the student to lay the trumpet on the lap, bell toward the left, with the second valve slide downward. Then I have the student pick up the trumpet, using the left index finger on the bell side of the third valve casing (supported by the middle finger, if necessary) and the thumb on the receiver side of the first valve casing, being sure to leave space between the palm of the hand and the valve casings. The ring finger of the left hand should be in the ring. Adjust an adjustable one so the ring rests against the bell side of the middle finger when the slide is closed. Use the back of the middle finger to push the slide out, and the inside of the ring finger to pull it back in. The pinky should rest next to the ring finger, rather than beneath the third slide (which can lead to distortions of the angle and pivot).

I have the student place the mpc gently into the receiver with the right hand, and turn it, gently, 1/4 turn just to seat it without applying any strength to the turn.

Now, using JUST the left hand I'll have the student repeat the previous steps to get a sound from the trumpet. If sufficient time has been spent on mouthpiece, lip compression and breathing practice, the first open note on the horn should be a second line "G."

Note: if the student's hand is too small to hold the trumpet at the proper angle with the left hand alone, I'll usually recommend using a cornet instead of a trumpet.

All of this, and we haven't even added the right hand yet!

Finally, we'll add the right hand. The tip of the thumb should be placed "in the cave" between the first and second valve casings and beneath the leadpipe. The pads of the first, second and third fingers rest comfortably on the valve buttons (there should exist a gentle sideways "C" or "U" between the first finger and thumb, depending on the size of the student's hand). The pinky finger should be free. I prefer not even to rest it upon the top of the ring at this point, telling the students that it is only used for applying a mute whilst playing, or holding the horn with one hand while turning a page of music and continuing to play.

TONGUE GAMES

Next we'll do some tongue games.

First, I'll have the students stick their tongues out of their mouths as far as possible (with the tip pointed as much as possible).

Then I'll have them try to touch the tip of their nose with their tongue; then their chin.

Then I'll have them wiggle their tongue side to side and up and down.

Finally, I'll have them touch the tip of the tongue gently to the inside of the lower lip and spit (like they're spitting out a watermelon seed or a cat hair). This is also helpful if they have trouble getting a buzz to start.

Now we'll apply the tongue start to the "G" we've already played. First, with whole notes, then halves, then quarters, then, if they can, eighths. (Sorry to those of you across the pond for the nomenclature: breves, semi-breves, quavers, etc)

We'll also take a break from holding the horn, learn how to hold it when not playing: (concert rest = bell on left knee, mpc up, right hand off) (lap =bell toward left, mpc toward right, to expedite picking up with left hand), and do some more mpc buzzing.

I'll also play a couple of examples of trumpet recordings for the students, both classical and jazz, by artists whom I believe to have characteristic trumpet sounds, such as Philip Smith, Maurice Andre for classical, Louis Armstrong, Dizzy Gillespie, or Clifford Brown for jazz.

And this is a first lesson for an absolute beginner. Practice assignment is to buzz lips alone three times a day, buzz mpc three times a day, play the "G" three times a day as a long note and as a tongued note, and do the "Bumblebee" (wiggle the valves as fast as possible while blowing any note into the trumpet).

At the second lesson, I introduce double-low pedal tones, played very gently, between buzzing the lips and mouthpiece and playing a "G" on the horn.

All of this is by way of explaining that trumpet playing is a science as well as an art, and that mastery of the basics is essential to reaching the stage where the finer points of interpretation can be addressed.

Sufficient time spent mastering the rudiments of trumpet playing lessens the need for in-depth remedial work later in the student's playing life.

It also helps to prevent the development of bad habits, which are so much harder to break!

ROLE OF THE TEACHER

There are <u>many</u> valid yet different approaches to trumpet playing/teaching basically because there is such DIVERSITY in players, playing styles, learning styles and teaching styles.

Do I teach the same "method" to every student who sits in my "hot seat" once they're beyond the beginner stage?

Nope. Not a CHANCE!

Do I use many of the same, <u>basic</u>, logical principles based on anatomy and physiology?

Yes, but the application of those principles can change drastically!

For example: for some students learning to buzz correctly is absolutely essential to maintaining lip membrane vibration; for some students buzzing leads to stiffness.

It depends a lot on the makeup of the individual's lip tissues.

For some students, pedals impede progress at their particular stage of development; for some students, pedals are essential to their development of air usage and lower lip engagement.

And these are just two of countless examples.

For example: for some students simply hearing me play an excerpt from an etude, solo, or ensemble piece is sufficient for them to "get it". For some students, we must tear the piece apart; analyze every phrase and note, mark in fingerings, dynamics (beyond what is written), breath marks, phrase marks, articulations, etc.

It all depends on the needs of the particular student. .

That bears repeating:

IT ALL DEPENDS ON THE NEEDS OF THE PARTICULAR STUDENT!

I don't know ANY experienced "professional" teachers who don't make the effort to match their teaching style to the learning style of the student with whom they are working at the time.

Someone observing me teach consecutive lessons might become very confused because I may not be using the same approach, teaching style, techniques, literature, embouchure, articulation, etc with each student. .

If I did, I wouldn't be doing my job as a teacher.

Lessons are like shoes: sometimes you can get by with a pair of shoes that doesn't quite fit; sometimes the wrong shoes can cause injury to your feet.

Sometimes a teacher that doesn't quite fit your learning style and/or needs may be still able to help you with some aspect of your playing; sometimes they will suggest something that, if followed, will cause a problem for you later on.

I tell ALL of my students: Listen to everything. Apply what works for you. Discard the rest.

That's probably about the ONLY slogan that I use all the time. .

Other advice I give is <u>very</u> student-specific!

There are certain aspects of playing the trumpet that are universal, in my humble opinion:

You must breathe before blowing (but the degree and intensity of that breathing must change, based upon what you are playing).

You must hold the trumpet in as relaxed a hold as possible (but that relative relaxation or tension can change, based upon how loudly or softly, or how high or low you must play).

You must have your lips in contact with each other and with the mouthpiece to produce a characteristic trumpet tone .

But so many other variables are just that: VARIABLES that change with every different player, every different playing situation, and every different piece of music or style of music played.

And as far as learning ONLY from "professional orchestral players," frankly, some of the greatest lessons I've learned in music came from folks who DIDN't sit "in the chair"! (And some didn't even play the TRUMPET!)

Don't limit yourself because you hold a bias, either FOR or AGAINST a particular type of player or teacher. You just might be surprised by the positive results you achieve by opening up your viewpoint!

TEACHING VIA SOUND

I often hear of teachers who believe that simply listening to a good sound will enable a student to produce a good sound themselves.

For some players this is true: all that is necessary is the simple demonstration of a particular sound or style, and the talented pupil is capable of reproducing the same.

But this is a gift (or talent, if you prefer). For some types of students, it IS necessary to explain in more detail.

Many students will struggle again and again with trying to accomplish playing a two octave C major or chromatic scale, but if their embouchure is totally incorrect, or even slightly incorrect because of incorrect mouthpiece placement or perhaps thrusting their tongue between their lips, they won't be able to accomplish their goal no matter how hard they try.

For much of my early life I had no formal trumpet instruction (merely participated in school band programs) and was largely self-taught, through much trial and error. I think I could have accomplished as much or more if I had had a thoughtful, thorough trumpet-playing teacher to save me from some of the mistakes that I might have avoided with good guidance.

When I finally DID take private lessons, in my senior year of high school, it was from a man who was doing his DMA in trumpet performance, and had spent a great deal of time thinking about pedagogy. It was from him that I first learned about H.L.Clarke, Claude Gordon, and the like; and I believe that, as a result of his input, I was able to achieve more progress in that one school year than I had in the previous nine years.

Some people believe that an excellent trumpet teacher "shouldn't burden the student with a million different things to think about."

An "excellent trumpet teacher" is one who enables the student to achieve the desired goals of being a good enough player to be able to produce MUSICAL sounds. This requires good tone quality, good technique, awareness of style and historical practice, and exposure to good literature.

Sound must be achieved; and if it were possible to create a sound merely by listening and emulating a good example, then there would be many more Bud Herseths and Louis Armstrongs and Maurice Andres than this world has yet seen.

But besides listening, achieving a great sound also requires the student's being able to analyze his or her own efforts in the practice room: patient correction of errors, attention to proper technique, posture and breathing, and the ability to formulate the questions that he or she wants to work through with the trumpet teacher.

Very frankly, part of my training as a teacher was learning to LISTEN to my students to diagnose difficulties, both to their PLAYING and to their DESCRIPTIONS of their own perceived difficulties.

Sometimes, those "perceived difficulties" are a matter of perception alone, and a simple verbal redirection is sufficient to get the student back on track (i.e.: someone who has a "GREAT day", over-practices as a result, injures their chops, and needs to take a bit of time off immediately, and then establish a regular, daily warmup/practice regimen). This is something that is easily helped via email, phone calls, or even a FAQ page, and doesn't need an "IN PERSON" lesson.

Sometimes the difficulties are greater than the student perceives and the task becomes one of helping the student get to the point of experiencing the feeling and physical activity that will correct the problem.

In either case, though in-person teaching is, granted, far EASIER than "Web-teaching", it is NOT the only option, and in some cases not an option at ALL!

Frankly, my whole approach to teaching, and I honestly believe the most ethical approach to ANY sort of teaching, once your student is beyond the beginning phase, or particularly for CP's (comeback players), is that of TEACHING THE STUDENT TO TEACH HIM/HERSELF.

Now, that might seem like an oxymoron to those who believe in the "Listen and Play as I Do" approach to teaching. (As Clint "Pops" McLaughlin has stated, this only works with a small percentage of students, and those are an even smaller percentage of ALL trumpet students, since those who are accepted into college as music majors have already reached a certain level of ability, and will most likely hit a brick wall plateau if their learning style doesn't jive with the "Listen and Play as I Do" approach).

Now think about it.

The most a trumpet teacher will see their individual students in a given week is a couple of hours. And that is only if they have a lesson AND a Master Class AND an ensemble together (many see their students only for a 30-45 minute lesson once per week).

The student must, if determined to succeed, spend a good 2-3 HOURS per DAY in the practice room (ergo 14-21 hours per week spent alone with the horn).

Thus the student is, on average, spending more than SEVEN TIMES as much time (at least) alone with his/her instrument as they are spending in the teacher's studio.

Sobering thought, isn't it? And humbling.

When I was much younger, I used to think that what I said and did in the studio made a major difference in my students' lives and trumpet-playing.

Eventually I learned that the very best I could do was to teach a student how to teach him/herself. Guide them in their approach to practice, assign them literature and etudes, advise them on reading material, play for and with them--of course! All of the above.

But what really began to make a difference (in my own approach to playing as well as the lessons I was imparting to my students) was when I acknowledged a few pertinent points, and tried to reinforce them on a regular basis:

First (and foremost):
Musical talent is a gift from God, which requires of the recipient that it be developed to the highest possible degree, and then shared for the common good.

Second:
Practicing without analysis is busywork, and leads to boredom, wasted effort, and the development of severe bad habits, instead of optimal growth.

Third:
The DAILY performance of a consistent warmup (repeated EVERY time the horn is played in a given day, though it might be shortened as necessary) is absolutely imperative to achieve consistency in playing response.

Fourth:
As long as equipment is not impeding the performance of necessary skills, it's ridiculous to go chasing after something new (it will waste time, money, AND effort spent adjusting to the new equipment which ALL could be spent better by making optimal use of what you already have!)

Fifth:
It's as important to listen to good performances (of many different types and instruments, not just by trumpeters) and experience the beauties of nature and of ALL the arts as it is to spend time in the practice room IF one aspires to becoming an <u>artist</u> in the truest sense of the word (that is, "one who creates that which is beautiful.")

Sixth:
Strive to play with the greatest possible ease and efficiency. Ride your air column as if it were a wave (and experience the JOY of that feeling). Keep your jaw, throat, shoulders, upper back arms, hands, etc as relaxed as possible. Keep your head aligned with your spinal column (investigate the ALEXANDER TECHNIQUE and apply it to your playing posture). Use your tongue, lips, jaw, hands, and air to afford yourself the greatest possible number of variations in style, timbre, attack, and release. In other words: expand your musical palette so that you can create the colors you want to express the music within you.

And finally: Remember to LOVE what you are doing. If it stops being a labor of love, take a break, go visit someone in the hospital or a nursing home, feed some animals at a shelter (or better yet, adopt one!), help out at a soup kitchen, etc. In other words: COUNT YOUR BLESSINGS! Do so every day, and offer up your efforts as a prayer. You'll be amazed at what a difference it can make.

And practice the gift of ENTHUSIASM!

Professor Ivan Galantic, PhD, Professor Emeritus of Tufts University, who now teaches for the Harvard Extension School, described the roots of enthusiasm as coming from the Greek word "Theos" or "God" when he spoke recently at the funeral of a friend.

"Therefore," he says, "to display enthusiasm is to bring out the God within us."

Sometimes all it takes for a child (or the child inside any of us) to succeed is for someone else to encourage him or her enthusiastically.

For many years, I've kept a big sign high up on the wall of my teaching studio with a simple, two-word message: ***"I CAN!"***

I don't allow my students to say, *"I can't."* It's okay for them to acknowledge that they haven't reached their goal yet; it's okay for them to know that they still have a ways to go. But, it's not okay for them to practice self-defeating behavior.

Think of the difference! Even by saying, *"I can't do it yet,"* you are allowing negativity to creep in. It's far better to say *"I'm progressing"* or even *"Every day, in every way, I'm getting a little bit better and better"* (thanks to Dr. Norman Vincent Peale).

Another concept that is helpful is to realize that your grasp never exceeds your reach. For example, if you want to grasp a pencil on the other side of your desk, but only reach a quarter of the way across the desk, you won't succeed. But if you reach beyond the end of the desk, grasping the pencil (which is merely on the other side) becomes an accomplished fact!

The same is true for trumpeters. Each of us must be our own, inner teacher in order to succeed (however you might define the term *succeed*). Your trumpet teacher/band director/colleagues are with you at best for scant hours every week, so their influence on you, though it may SEEM great, pales in comparison to the way you interact with your inner self on a daily basis.

How many times have you criticized yourself in a recent practice session? Oh, I'm not talking about *correcting* yourself--that's very important if you're going to improve. But have you treated yourself with the same sense of kindness and encouragement as you would, say, an 8 year old beginner?

I know you're not 8 years old, nor are you likely to be a beginner, but you still have the same sensitivity, deep within yourself, as you did when you were a youngster, or you wouldn't be very effective as a musical artist, would you?

You Are Your Own Best Teacher!

A few thoughts for you to consider adding to your *self-teaching* repertoire:

1. Always try three times (no matter what the task). If you have not succeeded by your third try, then take a break or move on to something else for the time being. You'll often succeed at your next session (or the following one), but if you keep pushing after three tries you may be tensing up and/or causing yourself injury. So try three times, and then give it a rest.

2. Record your practice sessions, and listen to them as if they were being played by a student (this isn't always necessary, but can give you some real insights if done, say, once a week or so).

3. Write down your observations and look at them in a day or two--- BUT make sure that your comments are phrased positively (as in *"First attack in the third movement needs to be clearer"* NOT *"First attack in the third movement STUNK!"*), and that you actively think about the best way to correct any mistakes (for example: *"Practice air attacks, then marcato, set the tongue before releasing air"*) Be as specific as you can.

4. Take some time every day for visualization: SEE yourself succeeding at your goals (See yourself performing confidently in front of an audience. See yourself confidently playing that technical passage in your solo. Hear your clear tone and clean attacks)

5. Listen to (and imitate) great artists, both on the trumpet and on other instruments (including voice). Analyze what makes their performances seem so effortless, so musical. How do they phrase? How do they connect their phrases? How do they release notes? Practice imitating those phrases, releases, etc.

6. Take a few minutes to do some deep breathing before you play. Breathe in deeply, thinking of the word *"HOME"* (let your mouth form the word as you inhale). Breathe out slowly, through gently closed lips (but not buzzing), and gradually increase the air speed by using your torso muscles. Repeat this several times before beginning your regular warmup.

There are other concepts that are equally helpful, but I urge you to be kind to yourself while practicing (which doesn't mean you can't also be *tough*!)

Be careful of trying to be too flamboyant. The goal, as Dan Patrylak would say, is not to have the audience appreciate how difficult it might be to perform a particular piece, but how easy you've made it appear.

It is the hard work of practicing and pedagogy that enables us to produce the best of playing, the best of music.

Be your own best teacher.

And share the gift of creating that inner self-teacher with your own students!

CHAPTER 18

A Word About Equipment

How Many Mouthpieces in Your Barrel?

There was once a very famous trumpet player who would trade mouthpieces with students who sounded good in a lesson. He would then take the student's mouthpiece home and practice on it for a few weeks before it, too, would land in one of the many barrels full of mouthpieces in his basement.

The mouthpiece game is like the myriad tourist traps that await the unwary traveler on the road to success!

Many, many a trumpeter has fallen victim to the "magic mouthpiece" myth.

"This mouthpiece will give you unlimited range, power, endurance."

"This mouthpiece will correct your embouchure difficulties."

"Use only a computer controlled design mouthpiece." "No! Only a hand-cut mouthpiece will do!"

No wonder so many trumpet players go crazy over mouthpieces!

Don't allow yourself to become neurotic about equipment: too many people rely on switching mouthpieces, horns, or supportive devices rather than learning how to play well on what they've already got!

Now that doesn't mean I don't believe in fitting a proper sized mouthpiece to a player! Or that one cannot use different mouthpieces for different types of work (one need not use the same mouthpiece for both piccolo and classical Bb or C trumpet work, for example).

Mouthpieces are like shoes: you can spend all kinds of money on designer labels, but in the end all that matters is protecting your feet from the elements!

And, yes, there are elements from which you need to be protected in trumpet playing, too!

For example: if you are required to be playing outside in cold weather, you might choose to make use of a plastic or Teflon rimmed mouthpiece, or even use one of the new Kelly plastic mouthpieces to keep your lips from freezing to the mouthpiece as you play.

If you have particularly thick, inflexible lips you might choose to play on a wider rim mouthpiece.

Players who are capable of playing with closed lips and rolled lips may be quite comfortable on smaller diameter rims and/or shallower cups.

Players who play with open lips may prefer a larger diameter rim and a deeper cup.

But not always!

The biggest difference I've noticed in my own playing is that playing on a smaller mouthpiece requires more inward rolling of the lip membrane (to keep the rim in the "white" muscle of the lip), whereas the use of a wider or deeper cup allows me to use more outward roll of the lips, enabling a darker sound.

The use of a wider aperture on a smaller mouthpiece can often create the "bottoming out" sensation, just as the use of a highly rolled in embouchure on a deeper cup can cause faster fatigue.

On the other hand, tonguing is often more difficult on a deeper cup mouthpiece because the process of tonguing causes a tremendous volume or velocity of air to strike the vibration point of the lips and causes them to open. The player's muscles must then re-close the lips. A very deep cup can create the sensation of a vacuum, which pulls the lips into the bowl.

The trumpeter's embouchure must be strong enough to re-close the lips and resist the pull of the deeper cup. Less-experienced players would be well-advised to stay with moderate sized, moderate depth mouthpieces for most playing applications.

In my experience, it's best to be as versatile as possible and learn to use both large diameter and small diameter rims, as well as both deep and shallow cups. It is important to remember, however, that learning to use a new mouthpiece takes a good deal of time, experimentation and repetition in order to learn the responses between your body and the mouthpiece.

Mel Broiles used to recommend setting all your trumpets and mouthpieces out on the table. Then play every combination of trumpet and mouthpiece on every excerpt or solo, and *make them all sound the same*!

The key to success with any equipment is learning to manipulate your body's response to the new sensations and stimuli generated by the interaction between the equipment and your body. This is complex, since you must align or coordinate existing muscle memory, instinct, habits and responses with the new stimuli.

For example: using a new mouthpiece produces a different feedback loop. On your familiar, long-term mouthpiece you play a note via a learned response. Ideally, you know exactly how much tongue and lip pressure, air quantity and air support to use to obtain the exact pitch, note length, dynamic level, articulation, and style the music requires.

On a new mouthpiece (or horn, for that matter), your usual, learned actions may elicit a dreaded "fraak" or a mis-tongued, mal-adjusted distortion of what you expected to play.

If you're like many players, one missed note leads to an increase in tension. This inevitably leads to more and more missed notes, more tension, and in worst-case scenarios, a pervasive fear of performing sets in.

If, instead, you make a quick analysis and adjustment to your approach (having, through sufficient practicing, developed a palette of techniques which can be applied), your attacks become surer and your focus more acute, leading to an even better performance!

Attitude is SO much of the formula to success.

Not long ago there was a thread on the Trumpet Players' International Network (TPIN) about "cheater mouthpieces." Let's explore that idea a bit, shall we?

"CHEATER MOUTHPIECES"

First of all, you really can't cheat by using a smaller mouthpiece (though you can <u>TRY</u> to), and those who believe that they can do so without having spent the requisite time on development are deluding themselves.

Let me explain: a smaller diameter rim and shallower cup offer no more advantages to playing in the upper register than does the piccolo trumpet. You really can't play any higher on the piccolo or the smaller mouthpieces than you can on a normally (and properly) sized mouthpiece.

Here is the reason: it actually takes MORE muscularity and control to play the smaller equipment than the larger equipment, at least, with a decent sound, good attacks, and good pitch.

Hence, those who attempt to use either the piccolo or smaller mouthpieces for extreme upper range soon find themselves "bottoming out", applying severe excess pressure, or simply being unable to produce any sound at all.

Younger players, consider this a warning: TINY MOUTHPIECES CAN DO DAMGE TO YOUR CHOPS IF YOU HAVEN'T DEVELOPED SUFFICIENT STRENGTH AND CONTROL TO PLAY THEM!

By the same token, mouthpieces that are too large can also damage your chops by forcing you to overblow or use excessive pressure to maintain a seal between your lips.

Often when players play on a mouthpiece which is too large for them, either in depth of cup (causing them to collapse their lips into the bowl of the mouthpiece) or in diameter (causing them to use excess pressure, close their teeth/throat, or lose range, control, or endurance or become fatigued easily), it is because they've been subjected to the demands of a director who has a misconception of the sound of a trumpet.

These same directors, given the choice of picking out their "ideal trumpet sound" are more likely to choose that of:

    A. A small-bore trombone in the upper register
    B. A cornet with a deep mouthpiece or
    C. A fluegelhorn.

Now, I have to say that I love the sound of a fluegelhorn, under certain circumstances, and there is nothing quite like the sound of an all-brass band, which distinguishes between trumpets, cornets, and fluegelhorns. However, in my humble opinion, to make a trumpet section sound totally dark (and usually quite un-centered, if the truth be known) is contrary to the principles and traditions of trumpet timbre.

Some people mistakenly believe that wider mouthpieces place added demands on endurance only at first, but if you stick with it, your body adapts. Over time, the endurance penalty fades.

Unfortunately, this isn't necessarily true. More often, the case is such that players jumping to inappropriately sized mouthpieces develop seriously bad habits, which can lead to injury, and even loss of playing ability.

Think of it in terms of shoe size. You wouldn't put a size thirteen shoe on a ten-year-old because it made his feet appear larger, and thus might be likely to make him look like a better basketball player, would you?

Or you wouldn't put adult-weight shoes on a pre-schooler in the hopes that he or she would develop stronger muscles (adapt) and thus become a better runner in the future, would you?

In both of the preceding examples, you'd be lucky if the child involved escaped serious injury. Yet band directors (and, regrettably, some trumpet teachers) persist in prescribing larger and larger mouthpieces for students, either in the mistaken impression that their sounds appear to be darker (in reality they're more often "deader", with less overtones in the timbre) OR that putting them on the largest available mpc will "straighten out any embouchure problems."

That's like attaching weights to the legs of a child with rickets or polio in the hopes that they'll develop stronger bones (when in reality their bones will probably break from the stress!)

It's far more responsible to assign a student a mouthpiece based on the following factors:

A. Age/length of study of the student
B. Overall size and shape of the facial muscles
C. Overall size and shape of lip tissues
D. Responsiveness of lip tissues (ease of vibration)
E. Tooth and jaw structure
F. Pivot and/or angle caused by tooth and jaw structure
G. Demands placed upon the student

Some folks also believe that a wider mouthpiece lets a wider section of the lips vibrate and contribute to the sound. Theoretically, this is true; however, it depends on the responsiveness of the lip tissue. Someone whose epithelial layer of lip tissue is highly cornified (thick, relatively dried out surface layer of skin on lips) is less likely to succeed with this sort of approach.

They may, in fact, do better with a mouthpiece that is smaller in diameter, deeper in cup, bigger in throat (but not backbore), and that has a wider, more rounded rim.

Someone whose lips are relatively thin, but very responsive could get away with playing on a very large rim or a very small rim, and could play deep or shallow, depending on their performance needs, the degree of practicing they've been doing, etc.

Some players believe that the effect of a deeper cup is not identical to the effect of a wider rim and that deeper cups lead to a mellower kind of dark sound, whereas a wider rim leads to a richer sound (dark without losing the harmonics, if that makes sense).

Again, depending on the lips themselves, the contrary may, in fact, be true. Richness of sound <u>does</u> stem from the presence of many overtones that are properly in tune with the fundamental, but this is usually best accomplished by rolling the red of the lips outward to a degree.

Shallower cups are more difficult to play with the Maggio style of rolling the lips outward (which tends to produce the additional overtones), but easier to play with lips that are rolled slightly inward. Perhaps the best possible sound is that of a slightly rolled-in embouchure, with a deeper cup, and an appropriately sized and shaped rim.

Deeper cups are easier to play with the Maggio rolled-out type of embouchure and more difficult to play with lips rolled in (since there is more of a tendency to feel the lips collapsing into the bowl with a deeper cup.)

An option, which may be preferable, is that of opening the throat of the mouthpiece (and not necessarily the backbore, though backbores can also assist in coloring the sound). Thus, the mouthpiece will feel like it can take more air, but the lips needn't feel like there's a vacuum in the bowl (if it's deeper), nor that they will "bottom-out" if the cup is shallower.

A successfully set-up embouchure is more likely to succeed, whatever the equipment available.

A poorly fit mouthpiece is likely to derail even relatively good chops, if care is not taken to pay attention to the process of playing in a way that will not "give-in" to the particular traps of whatever that particular mpc might be.

For some players there is never a need to even consider equipment: they are able to "just play" or "just judge approach via the sound produced."

But for far many more players it becomes very important to ensure that the match between anatomy, physiology and equipment is made carefully and responsibly.

In fact, often the source of many players' frustrations is a mismatch between their physical characteristics, the embouchure they were taught to use, and the mouthpiece they use.

This is a very good reason for teachers to become familiar with the anatomy and physiology of the embouchure, as well as literature, technical approaches, and stylistic considerations. It's important that teachers do not just operate on the "listen and imitate" or "do as I say, not as I do" or "just tongue and blow, kid" approaches. A teacher must match their teaching style to the learning style of the student, and must assist with the fitting of proper equipment for the particular student's needs.

As I've mentioned before, there are some "naturals" who are able to surmount any difficulties by virtue of sheer time spent in the practice room, but not everyone is so blessed.

Let me give you an analogy: when we first learn to write we learn to write huge letters on wide lines with a very thick pencil. As we gain better control of our fine motor skills, we progress to smaller writing implements and (hopefully) are able to write legibly with smaller sized characters.

You'll find, also, that though some experienced players, particularly those of us who play both sides of the horn (classical/symphonic and commercial/jazz), are able to switch rim sizes when a different tone color is desired, or simply to make easier the job of playing long hours in the extreme upper register over a loud ensemble. However, I suspect, with a little further investigation you'll discover that these same players are capable of playing in the same range on their larger, symphonic piece as they are with the smaller piece (it just requires a bit more work).

When it comes to range and <u>power</u> development (which is the <u>REAL</u> issue in so-called "range" development), there is no substitute for proper mechanics. In other words: proper mouthpiece size and placement, proper usage of anatomy and physiology (that is, the use of your body and <u>how</u> you use it), and proper use of air (both in terms of volume/quantity and velocity/speed) are all important factors.

Once you have learned to play optimally, you should be able to play any style, and any range, in any volume or dynamic, requiring any particular technical demands (such as double or triple tonguing, for example) on <u>ANY</u> mouthpiece.

Until you have spent sufficient time mastering the basics, however, you risk permanent damage to your chops by forcing them to tackle tasks for which they have not been prepared.

Would you send a talented junior high school football player out onto the field with adult, professional linebackers? Maybe he'd do okay for a while (if he could run very fast), but eventually he'd get tackled and the damage could be fatal.

Don't take the risk. Believe me, trumpet playing can be with you for your entire lifetime (I have colleagues and students in their 90's who are still playing and loving it!), and the time you spend practicing will pay off (and go faster than you'd ever believe possible.)

Patience is a virtue for range and power development, friends, just as it is in so many other areas of life, and a few extra months of rational work-outs will yield far better results than the crutch of a mouthpiece that isn't appropriate to your stage of development.

ADJUSTING TO A DEEPER CUP

On the other side of the coin is the adjustment to playing on a deeper cup. Usually a player will make use of a deeper cup mouthpiece in order to blend a relatively bright sound with the darker sounds around him or her in a section. Some soloists will choose a deeper cup for a darker timbre as well.

Do be careful, though, about confusing a "darker sound" with a sound lacking in overtones (what we call a "dead sound").

In order to play on a very deep mouthpiece, it is important to have a strong enough embouchure to re-secure or re-close the lips after the attack has caused them to open.

Tonguing may be more difficult because tonguing causes the lips to open and a deep cup creates a sort of vacuum, which may cause the lips to collapse into the bowl of the cup.

Weaker or less-experienced players should avoid using very deep cups until their pout control and lip roll is well-developed. Isometric exercises can assist with this process.

MOUTHPIECE THROATS

Vacchiano used to recommend using a size "24" throat, although he preferred the "22" throat for ease of response.

I have played on a throat as large as an "11", but prefer the "22" throat myself for most applications.

The average mouthpiece tends to have about a "28" throat, though some mouthpieces go as small as a size "32."

In this situation, no one can really advise you but Lady Experience! You need to try some different throat sizes with your horn or horns and decide which size gives you the best response for the type of playing you must do.

EQUIPMENT MAINTENANCE

It goes without saying that you should keep your mouthpiece and mouthpiece case clean. Avoid playing after eating. If you must play after a meal, at least take the time to swish your mouth out with water to avoid blowing particles of food into the mouthpiece and lead pipe of your horn.

Try to have at least one extra copy of your main mouthpiece. Mouthpieces are susceptible to damage, loss or theft. You would be well-advised to be prepared with a spare!

Flush your horn out at least once per week; and give it a full bath once per month. Re-lubricate all the slides and valves.

I like *Zaja* slide grease and *Al Cass Fast* valve oil best.

Wrap your horns in an old t-shirt or felt bag before placing in the case and they will keep their finish longer.

A SPECIAL ARBAN'S TRICK FOR LONG-LIFE

I've found it particularly helpful with the soft-bound edition of Arban's Complete Conservatory Method to break the binding and punch three holes in each page.

It's also helpful to place o-ring hole-reinforcers on each punched hole. Then I place the pages in a loose-leaf binder.

This way the book lasts much longer!

MOUTHPIECE SOUND SLEEVES/TONE ENHANCERS

Several different manufacturers produce these devices, which are designed to reduce extraneous vibration in your mouthpiece shank and focus the vibrations in the cup of the mouthpiece.

Whether or not you will feel a difference in your playing by using one is truly a matter of personal preference. Some players are so sensitive to the "feel" of their equipment that the slightest change of any variable is acutely noticeable to them.

Other players notice no difference at all.

Several manufacturers produce these, including Mark Curry, but I especially like the ideas of young Josh Landress (www.jlandressbrass.com) who uses wood to create a very interesting effect in his brass *"Ultra-Sleeve."*

I encourage you to contact him directly: 516-521-7101 to arrange to try the device. I've noticed an improvement in some students' attacks that seems to be directly attributable to the use of this *Ultra-Sleeve*.

You'll have to judge for yourself.

WEIGHTED SLIDES/HEAVY CAPS/HEAVY BRACES

Same thing as the tone enhancers: it's all up to the individual player's sensitivity and personal taste.

Some believe that these make a huge difference; some believe they make a slight difference. Some notice no difference at all.

I tell my students over and over: Listen to everything. Apply what works for you. Discard the rest.

This also applies to equipment, with a caveat: don't waste your time on new equipment if you're ready, willing, and able to devote the necessary time to master it! In the end, it seems, most gadgets wind up in the junk drawer.

Caveat emptor! (Buyer Beware!)

CHAPTER 19

Navigating the Jungle

(Avoiding Professional Pitfalls)

The following are lessons I've learned through nearly 40 years of professional performance life. I hope these lessons may save you from some of the difficulties that many of us have experienced out in the jungle of professional music performance.

1. BE GRACIOUS TO AUDIENCE AND COLLEAGUES

I remember well the aftermath of a recital with which I was not particularly pleased. Though I felt I could have done better, the audience was still enthusiastic and wanted to come backstage and congratulate me.

I was very young, and called for my teacher to come advise me. How should I respond to the comments of the audience?

His response was simple and to-the-point:

"Say 'Thank-you for coming. I'm glad you enjoyed it!' Don't make any excuses, or explain how you think you might have done better. Most of the people in the audience have no idea that you didn't perform as well as you wanted. They enjoyed the performance and want to share their experience of it with you."

Think back to the last time you gave a performance that didn't meet your expectations. Were you gracious and grateful to the audience, or did you act out your disappointment (or even anger) on your colleagues and, perhaps, some of the audience members?

Of course, each of us sets out to make every performance as perfect as possible; but real life is imperfect and sometimes things occur that are beyond our control.

If, when we make a mistake, we become upset with ourselves and lose our concentration, that single mistake is likely to multiply like a warren of rabbits!

If, on the other hand, we acknowledge the mistake (for future reference), but move on as if it did not occur, the rest of the performance may exceed our expectations because the mistake heightened our awareness and caused us to focus more acutely on the task at hand.

2. KEEP A POSITIVE ATTITUDE

Attitude can be a deciding factor in whether or not you get hired (or hired back).

One of my adult students has an interesting addition to his business card: "A Pretty Nice Guy"<!>

Well, he IS a pretty nice guy! A true gentleman, who is kind and caring to his colleagues, and gets LOTS of calls for gigs--ALL THE TIME!

Every action, every word, and every glance you make on a gig or in a rehearsal is noted by someone. Make sure that what they remember is your honest, kind, caring and professional nature and you will enjoy a long association with that organization.

Many years ago, when I first came to Boston, I played in a lot of rehearsal groups in order to make contacts with other musicians. One of those groups was a rehearsal big band with many area professionals who played in it during the quiet part of the year.

I was playing lead trumpet, and on one particular piece the person playing 2nd trumpet/jazz was not following the articulation marks during a shout chorus. I leaned over during a quick rest and said "shorter!"

Well...to this day, that trumpeter will turn and walk the other way when he sees me coming. We recently played a gig together for a big band in New Hampshire, and though he didn't walk off the bandstand, he literally *turned the other way while we were playing!*

In retrospect, I've come to realize that I should have waited until the break to talk to him about articulation. Sometimes there isn't much time on a gig to communicate, and people can misunderstand your motivation for saying something.

Giving a colleague a compliment before offering constructive criticism may pave the path to lasting friendship and cooperation.

3. BEWARE OF THE CONTRACTOR-WOLF

This predatory species can be deadly to your professional life. If you respond to his/her advances in a negative fashion, he/she may choose to blackball you:

> "I guess Jane Doe is an all right technician, but her *musicality* leaves something to be desired."

(It's hard to argue with this sort of judgment; so many folks just choose not to use the party in question).

If you respond to their advances in a positive fashion, she/he may take advantage of your naiveté for a while, but soon tire of you and chase after some other innocent young thing.

So what's a player to do?

One of the best things you can do is make sure that you are never, NEVER alone with a questionable contractor! (Ask around, these contractors get a reputation, and colleagues will be subtle but informative if you ask.)

If colleagues always surround you, you'll have witnesses to back you up.

If the unthinkable happens and you get cornered, be as graceful as possible extricating yourself from the situation. Call out to another player passing by (even if imaginary!), and apologize that you have to run and ask about another gig.

Then make a point of notifying the union about the incident. You don't necessarily have to file charges, but protect yourself by making the issue known.

4. SPECIAL CONSIDERATIONS FOR FEMALE TRUMPETERS

Besides being wary of the contractor-wolves, here are a few more considerations that apply to females in particular:

Be sure to dress properly for rehearsals and gigs: save the "vamp" outfits for nights out on the town, not professional situations. Don't show too much leg, chest, shoulder, or back.

Also be subtle in your application of makeup: less is more!

In a pinch, mascara on your lashes and brows may be enough. (Also, be careful of base makeup since some, which are sulfa-based, may interact with the silver-plating on your mouthpiece and turn your upper lip black!)

Over-prepare to circumvent misogynistic bias. If you are at the same level or slightly better than the male sitting next to you be prepared to play second to him all night long.

Be a lady. Avoid being "one of the guys." Don't tell dirty jokes or use inappropriate language.

Avoid dating colleagues or students. There are <u>very</u> rare exceptions to this rule, but in general: "Meat and money do not mix!" (Courtesy of my dear friend, Jimmy James, long-time ringmaster of the Beatty-Cole Circus).

Be sure your skirt is long enough to cover your knees when you are seated.

Check your nylons for runs before putting them on and carry some clear nail polish to stop runs that occur during a gig. (A drop of clear nail polish at the start of a run will keep it from continuing).

Check with the contractor/personnel manager about dress for females. Ladies do not always wear all black when gentlemen are wearing tuxedos.

Check to find out what the particular ensemble is asking its ladies to wear in performance and acquiesce in your own dress.

Beware of lipstick: some brands may cause your lips to dry and crack which can be disastrous for a trumpet player. Some brands will smear if you wear them while playing. In general, I find it's best to avoid wearing lipstick when playing—better to put it on AFTER the gig!

Be judicious in the amount and type of cologne or perfume you wear on gigs. Some colleagues may be sensitive to strong odors. It's better to smell like soap than a strong perfume.

THE "SO OBVIOUS THEY'RE OFTEN OVERLOOKED" GUIDELINES

Remember: the audience sees you before they hear you, so dress well and carry yourself well.

Groom yourself well, even for rehearsals. Be sure your body and hair are clean; use deodorant (preferably unscented); brush your teeth, shave, use mouthwash, dress cleanly and neatly. This demonstrates respect for your colleagues, the conductor, the music, the audience, and yourself!

Realize that your reputation precedes you: a good impression lasts, but one faux pas can follow you (and precede you) for decades!

Be attentive during rests: LISTEN to everyone else, and COUNT measures of rest (don't rely on others to count for you!)

BUT also know the music well enough to respond if there is an error (such as a conductor forgetting a repeat, a singer missing a cue, etc.)

Get sufficient rest before performances (and even rehearsals): you'll be more alert, contribute more, and be more accurate.

Arrive early to rehearsals and gigs (at least 30 minutes before the downbeat, more if you are unsure of the location and/or parking, or if it's the first time you're playing with a group).

Check beforehand on the literature to be played so you can bring the right instrument and accessories (not to mention play through the pieces if they're not in your working repertoire!)

Always bring your own valve oil. (Worst-case scenario: I was performing at a national convention, got on stage, and realized I'd forgotten my valve oil back in the dressing room. I borrowed some oil from a neighbor. It turned out to be synthetic oil which froze my valves solid. I wound up having to play on an exhibit horn for the performance.)

Always bring an extra music stand (just in case).

Don't use any alcohol or recreational drugs before a rehearsal or performance and be cautious about using over-the-counter and/or prescription drugs, which can impede your ability to think quickly and respond to the music and conductor.

Know the music and style well (avoid sight-reading on a gig unless absolutely necessary). Remember: you need to play MUSIC not just notes.

Dress in layers for outside gigs. (Once I had to play a gazebo gig at an ocean-side park in the early evening. An easterly breeze caused a fog to arise and chilled us all thoroughly. Luckily, I had an extra sweater under my jacket!)

Be sure you know what the required dress code is for a gig. If the dress is tuxedo/formal, make sure you have the appropriate blouse/shirt and tie. Don't wear a button-down shirt or a clip-on bowtie. Be sure to use a cummerbund (gentlemen) and to have a long enough skirt to cover your knees when sitting (ladies).

Polish your shoes!

Bring sunglasses, sunscreen, windscreen/clips, and possibly a hat for outdoor gigs. Be careful of bug sprays and insecticides, which could be harmful to colleagues with breathing difficulties.

Never wear strong perfume/cologne/aftershave to a gig. Personal scents should always <u>whisper</u> (not shout!).

You may find that placing single pieces of music on the stand will work better than an entire folder, particularly if you have a wire stand.

Unless you are a principal or lead player, do NOT tell others how to play something, and NEVER presume to advise someone else if you are a substitute.

Do NOT tap your foot! (Jazz gigs are an exception…) Tapping your foot insults the conductor, interferes with your colleagues, annoys the audience, and is, in general, rude!

For those of you who absolutely cannot stop tapping your foot:
> Create a cushion out of an auto car-wash sponge, covered in black fabric. Place the cushion under the offending foot<!!>

Don't talk during rehearsals, unless you're a principal or lead player giving direction (and even then keep it short, quiet and to-the-point!)

Beware of electronic tuners: use your ears and don't assume that your pitch is correct. Always be ready and willing to adjust.

Tune to the first violins in an orchestra, the clarinets in a band, and the bass in a jazz ensemble.

Please DON'T use vibrato in unison passages!

Be aware that keyboards operate with "tempered" pitch, not true or "just" intonation and modify your intervals accordingly.

See the following link for more information about intonation: http://abel.hive.no/trumpet/resources/intonation/

Don't be afraid to mark your music. Even the great Mel Broiles would mark in fingerings, repeat signs, coda marks, etc. when preparing to read new music in a studio session.

Don't program literature as a solo that you don't know (and love) intimately.

By the same token, don't program music that is beyond your physical abilities.

Avoid dress rehearsals right before a performance. Too often people perform the performance at the dress rehearsal and have nothing left (physically, emotionally or spiritually) for the actual performance. Even dress rehearsals on the same day, but several hours previous to the performance can deplete you.

SPECIAL COMMERCIAL CONSIDERATIONS

Never sit in the lead chair on a gig until the leader tells you to do so. Always ask, even if you were hired to play lead. Be gracious if you are asked to move over for another player.

Never assume that a player who sits next to you is not as good as you. You can always learn something from everyone!

DON'T use vibrato on unison passages!

Always return to the stand promptly after a break. Be early or the first back, never the last.

Watch comments on the stage: many performers have been embarrassed to realize that a mike was live when they heard themselves say something inappropriate over the system.

Learn how to use microphones well, and be aware of how to turn them on and off properly. Beware of microphones without switches!

Befriend your sound technicians: they can make you sound very good or very bad!

Always carry clean, neat, unmarked business cards, but never give out a personal card to patrons when you're hired by a leader/contractor as a sideman or even lead player. Always refer patrons to the leader.

Same goes for "taking requests." Send them to the leader.

Same goes for accepting tips: they go to the leader who decides how and if to distribute them.

Never bring drinks onto the stand (except for bottled water).

Never eat on the stand, and never help yourself to food until invited by the host and okayed by the leader.

Always be gracious. Look for ways to compliment others. Accept positive feedback humbly and negative feedback gracefully.

Always thank the leader/contractor for the gig (both on the gig and afterwards).

Always ask for and encourage feedback.

Never overplay the lead or principal player if you are in a section. Mel Broiles used to tell an anecdote about playing in a section for a well-known big band leader who employed many high-register notes. Mel played a higher note than that leader at the end of a tune on a gig. Mel never was asked to play for that leader again.

Beware of criticizing colleagues. Even if it's constructive, criticism can back-fire with a sensitive colleague.

Avoid negative attitudes: Be positive and contribute to making the musical experience work well for everyone involved: the audience, your colleagues, and yourself.

Leave personal problems, grudges, anger, anything negative outside the hall. Negativity has no place in creative music. If you're feeling negative it will come through in your playing.

Never take a passage 8va or 8vb unless asked to do so.

Observe dynamics as written, but temper them to the size of the hall, the size of the ensemble and the ambient acoustics. Play in balance.

Know the music and your role in it. (Analyze!) Are you melody, harmony, fanfare, accent, color, special effect, rhythm, etc? Play accordingly.

PRACTICALITIES

Always bring a small bottle of water with you. Dehydration weakens your chops, especially in hot or humid conditions.

Keep a small tube of toothpaste in your case. It can help alleviate dry mouth.

Use sugar free gum if you have dry mouth.

Gly-Oxide works wonders for canker sores. (Don't use straight peroxide, because it can burn the mucous membrane) 8-10 drops and swish. Repeat 3-4 times per day for 3-4 days and the canker will be gone in most cases.

Avoid products containing camphor or menthol, which tend to cause the top layer of lip to dry out. Also beware of lanolin, which can cause allergic reactions in some people. Substitute Lip Rescue (which has tea tree oil), Chop Saver, or Vitamin A & D Ointment.

Stay healthy: eat well, take vitamins (Even if you think you eat well you may not always assimilate the vitamins and minerals you need from your food, particularly if you're feeling stressed.)

Avoid diet, carbonated beverages before a performance. Besides caffeine, they are also often high in sodium, which can increase your dehydration from blowing.

Have a Power Bar or other protein plus carbohydrate food bar before the performance. Drink plenty of water afterwards.

Eat a meal of complex carbohydrates and light protein approximately 2 ½ to 3 hours before the performance (to allow time for digestion).

Take a nap and put your feet up for about 30 minutes about an hour before you do your warm-ups.

Recognize the adrenaline rush/butterflies in your stomach feeling as a good thing that leads to a peak performance.
Some players find that taking beta-blockers helps to alleviate performance anxiety. Be careful: some may have undesirable side effects. Check with your doctor and don't take unfamiliar medications right before a performance.

Try high-dose B vitamins or herbal supplements. Natural is always best.

Avoid salty and or spicy foods before playing since they can cause swelling of the mucous membranes.

And finally:

Remember the JOY of performing and share it with your colleagues and the audience!

CHAPTER 20

"Give it BACK! It's Mine!"
A Philosophy of Trumpet Playing

How does one repay the gift of talent? For many people the question never even arises, but I'd like to challenge you to take a different tack.

Practice an attitude of gratitude and you'll experience a level of satisfaction with your playing that may be unprecedented in your previous experience.

Allow yourself to feel energy pouring through you, through your instrument and out to the members of the audience. You'll feel a connection and a returning energy that will invigorate you! And realize that you will project what you are feeling to the audience: keep it positive!

There is a parable that talks about a landowner who is going away on a trip. He calls three faithful servants and provides each of them with a bag of coins (called "talents"). When he returns, he asks each of them to account for their use of the talents.

The first servant had invested his talents, and caused them to increase several-fold in value. The landowner was greatly pleased, and doubled the amount the servant had raised as a gift for his diligence.

The second servant had attempted to invest his talents in crops, but lost all of them to bad weather and insects. The landowner rewarded his attempts by replacing the original amount he had received.

The third servant had buried his talents in a hole in the ground, and returned them to the landowner unchanged and unused. The landowner grew angry, threw the servant into jail, and confiscated the remaining talents.

The moral of the story: it is better to attempt to develop talents than to leave them unused.

Give thanks for everything: those things that are near perfect as well as those things that you would like to forget!

Soon you'll find that your joys outweigh your regrets by far.

Also, find ways to bring joy to others through your musical abilities.

Perhaps you might donate an hour or two per week to performing for a nursing home, veterans' center, or senior citizens' center. Music has amazing healing powers.

I remember one particular time I played a grueling duo performance at a nursing home with particularly challenging clients, several of whom were suffering from dementia (or what is now called *Alzheimer's*).

Usually nursing home performances had people singing along, sometimes even dancing to our traditional jazz, swing, and show tunes, but this time there was only one person who at first hummed, then sang along with us.

Later, as I was packing up, a nurse approached me.

"Did you know that *"A"* (a client in a secured wheelchair) doesn't even know her own last name any more? But she was singing every word to 'Alice Blue Gown'!"

The next time we returned to that home, the same nurse informed us that *"A"* had 'stayed with us' for hours following the performance.

This is only one example of an occurrence that we experienced frequently with the *Alzheimer's* population.

Perhaps you might offer coaching to music students at a local elementary school, or even run a collection drive for used musical instruments to be used by underprivileged children.

Nothing compares to the light in the eyes of a child who realizes that she/he is responsible for the beautiful (or not so beautiful yet!) sound coming from an instrument. Often, a battered, well-used instrument can make a major difference in a child's life by giving them a community of musical friends that will last a lifetime!

Perhaps you might choose to perform at a local church once per month (or even several different churches). Often you'll find that donating a service here or there will lead to your being offered paying gigs at holiday services or wedding ceremonies.

One advantage to church audiences: even very young children are affirmed by sharing their gift with the congregation because church members are seldom, if ever, critical of honest efforts.

You might also consider becoming a member of "Buglers Across America" which provides live buglers (trumpet players) to play "Taps" at military veterans' funerals (instead of the fake bugle CD players that the government provides, which is a travesty in my humble opinion since the veterans served in person, not by holograph!). (See www.baa.org)

Or maybe you will find your calling in being a teacher to others.

I did, and I give thanks every day for the blessings given me by my students!

Remember: the best way to learn something is to attempt to teach it to someone else.

Give back the gift…Pass the torch…Share the blessings.

It's the surest way to ensure that those blessings and gifts will grow--exponentially!

CHAPTER 21

Trumpet Tributes
The Trumpet Family Tree

You, by virtue of reading this book, are part of the trumpet family tree of Jeanne Gabriel Pocius,

Who is a student of:

Robert Lemons, student of Roger Voisin, student of Rene Voisin, Marcel LaFosse and Georges Mager (and Director of Bands at Eastern Connecticut State University)

&

William Vacchiano, student of Signor Di Nobili, Frank Knapp, Louis Kloepfel, Walter M. Smith, and Max Schlossberg (and Principal Trumpet of the New York Philharmonic Orchestra)

&

Melvin Broiles, student of William Vacchiano (and Principal Trumpet of the Metropolitan Opera Orchestra)

&

Jerome Callet

&

Daniel Patrylak, student of Sidney Mear and David Melson (and Solo Cornet with United States Marine Corps Band, "the President's Own" and founder of Eastman Brass Quintet)

Besides these applied teachers, I've also been blessed with many sage mentors who have inspired me as a performer, a writer, and a teacher-philosopher.

CATHERINE AMIR WADE was the orchestra director at my high school, Windham High School, in Willimantic, Connecticut, for many years. Catherine also worked tirelessly to teach literally thousands of students in elementary schools throughout the district. She worked miracles and never gave up hope, even in the face of many obstacles. I still cherish the opportunity to speak with her about my students and my performances.

EDWARD GERRY directed the summer junior orchestra in my town. He also conducted the Willimantic City Band, a union concert band, and played in the Maurice Bergeron Dance Orchestra, with which I performed in my teens. Ed was a pioneer in teaching instrumental music and jazz to developmentally delayed students (who were regarded in those days as being "mentally retarded"). Ed's tolerance, sensitivity and good humor continue to be an inspiration to me today, though he has been gone from this world for many years.

PHIL LANORMANDIN was a staple of the New York Brass Conference for Scholarships for many years, and well-known for his famous questions about breathing, tonguing, breath support, etc.: "I been meanin' to ask ya..." Phil studied trumpet with me until his breathing issues (late in life) forced him to retire (largely due to complications from colon cancer). His copious notes from many years of attendance at brass clinics and master classes are a great resource, which I hope to make available to the trumpet world. I play regularly on the antique, rotary-valve fluegelhorn he gave me several years before he passed away.

FATHER JOSEPH JOHN DAVID KUGLER, a Roman Catholic priest, first came into my life when I was playing with the folk mass group at my home parish. His eyes lit up at the thought of a trumpet soloist in the church, and he soon began to challenge me with transcriptions by Marie-Claire Alain and Maurice Andre (which I had to play on the regular Bb trumpet, since I didn't have a piccolo trumpet at that time). I credit my "Pepe" with the strong range and endurance I enjoy to this day, as well as my sight-reading acumen, since he would frequently bring brand new music to me for performance at Sunday Masses (that had nothing in common with our Saturday night rehearsals!). I still mourn his loss from this life.

HARRY JAMES was one of the kindest and greatest musician trumpeters it has ever been my honor to meet and to hear. I first met Harry when I was 12 years old, and he stayed in touch via Christmas and birthday cards and itineraries until he passed away. Harry's sound in person was the biggest, fullest and richest trumpet sound I have ever heard to this day! He also had a technique that would have served him well even in a symphony orchestra, had he chosen to pursue that route. Too many trumpeters judge him on the basis of the vibrato that is evident in some of his recordings, but that, too, evolved over the years he played. Harry doesn't get the credit he deserves for being one of the great technicians and jazz artists of his day.

BRUCE BELLINGHAM was the director of the UCONN Collegium Musicum when I was a student. Bruce's attention to details of phrasing and nuance of articulation on Renaissance instruments are a strong part of my performance palette. Bruce is also a strong bass player, and I enjoyed playing a wide variety of gigs with him over the years I lived in Connecticut. Bruce and his late wife, Patty, were dear and supportive friends to me when my son was very young.

JERRY LASZLOFFY was my conducting mentor from my junior year of high school through undergraduate study and well into my 20's. Jerry's focus on the accuracy of technique and application of technique to musicality is a foundation for my teaching and performance to this day.

ALLAN GILLESPIE was the Director of Bands at UCONN during my undergraduate study, but I also played for him at Laurel Music Camp. It was Allan's push that got me to audition for Vacchiano. Allan was a great teacher who inspired many successful students, including Larry Rachleff (Director of Bands at Rice University) and Tom Duffy (Director of Bands at Yale University), as well as many professional performers and music educators. Allan's concepts of phrasing and articulation are included in my palette approach to trumpet performance.

JEFF HOLMES, besides being a great jazz musician and composer, is also a fine trumpeter and trumpet teacher. Jeff's emphasis on internal phrasing and dynamics and accuracy in reading both jazz and classical continue to inspire me.

ROLF SMEDVIG is one of the truly unsung heroes of trumpet playing. Rolf is a musician's musician, whose tone, technique and interpretation are akin to that of the greats of all time! His work with the Armando Ghitalla foundation will ensure that the teaching and tradition of the Ghitalla School of trumpet playing will continue well into the next generations.

ROBERT LEMONS, DMA, was my first actual trumpet playing applied teacher and first introduced me to many of the standard trumpet texts including Claude Gordon, and Herbert L. Clarke. He also first introduced me to the works of Hovhannes, Arutunian, and Hindemith. Yet, Bob's basic humility and grace was such that he deferred to Vacchiano constantly. Bob is still Director of Bands at Eastern Connecticut State University.

DR. CHARLES COLIN, Founder of the New York Brass Conference for Scholarships, first brought me to New York City to perform as a soloist at the Conference. Through many of the succeeding years, we enjoyed countless hours of consultation about music and musicians (most occurred on my front porch over a glass of Coke, with Charlie's dear friend, Phil LaNormandin, sitting nearby). I still cherish the insights he gave me into the business of music and cherish the trumpet his beloved son, Alan, created. The MAX trumpet continues to be the finest trumpet I have ever played!

ROBERT "BO" WINIKER spent countless hours coaching me on authentic big band and early jazz styles. Bo is my brother in every way but blood! He's also one of the great unsung jazz trumpeters, who not only can channel just about any historic trumpeter you can name, but also is incredibly creative in his own right!

EDWARD "EDDIE" WINIKER became my father in music and in life. For many years I stood by the side of his piano in his combo and learned from a master musician and a consummate human being. Ed's infectious enthusiasm for music and people continues to inspire me in every performance I give. The saddest day of my entire life was the day I served as his pallbearer and played him to eternal rest with "A Trumpeter's Lullaby."

HAYR SOURP OSHAGAN MINASSIAN, a high priest of the Armenian Apostolic Church, has been one of the most inspiring persons it has ever been my honor to know. Father Minassian is founder and conductor of the Erevan Choral Society and Orchestra, choir director of Holy Trinity Armenian Apostolic Church, and my personal spiritual (and Armenian language) mentor. After breaking his neck in a diving accident when he was 25 years old, Father Minassian completed his Master's degrees in Musicology and Theology, his doctorate of Theology, and most of the work for his DMA in music! His repertoire of clean jokes is legendary, not only because the jokes are so funny, but also because he has them categorized so that he always has just the right joke to tell at the right time. I credit the miracle of healing that occurred with the tumor in my neck to Hayr Sourp and his beloved mother, Dira Mayr Sirvart Minassian.

WILLIAM VACCHIANO, besides being one of the greatest trumpet players of all time, was one of the simplest and kindest human beings I ever met. Vacchiano's approach to phrasing and articulation, his method for transposition by clef, his melodic and singing nature combined to make him the inspiration for generations of trumpet players as well as every other musician, conductor and audience member who ever listened to him play. I still marvel every time I listen to recordings of his playing. No other trumpet player of his generation ever approached his sound, technique, musicality, and artistry!

MEL BROILES, besides being a great trumpet player, was a very practical man. In many of our lessons, he focused on the skills needed to survive in the music world. Sight reading was key, as was the ability to perform well in a variety of styles and on a variety of instruments. To this day, recalling his performance of the trumpet solo from "Parsifal" brings chills to my spine and tears to my eyes. Mel has left a wonderful legacy of compositions, including his duets books, and many etude books and trumpet solos. I miss his smile.

JEROME CALLET is one of the great unsung heroes of the trumpet world. As a kid growing up in Pittsburgh, Jerry Callet practiced hours every day, and learned to tongue and transpose and play many orchestral excerpts well. When he was in his late teens he realized that he was not able to access his upper register (high C's were beyond a wall); and he consulted many trumpet teachers in an attempt to discover the reasons for this impediment. Jerry auditioned for Vacchiano and was rejected because he could not slur from low c to high C. This was a tremendous set-back for a determined young man who vowed to gain that upper register, regardless of the time, expense or effort required. Eventually, through the examination of live trumpeters and photographs of great trumpeters actually playing, Jerry developed his "Superchops" concept and began to teach it and to develop mouthpieces and eventually horns that would make it easier to play.

Throughout the entire process, Jerry has remained humble and self-effacing in person. Jerry is sincerely interested in furthering knowledge about the trumpet and trumpet playing and in helping trumpeters overcome challenges facing them, be they the adjustment to false teeth (which has brought him several name symphonic players who've sought help discretely) or the recuperation from serious lung injury (which was how I personally became acquainted with Jerry's unique kindness and attentiveness). In short, you'd be hard-pressed to find a more sincerely enthusiastic trumpet player and student of the science of trumpet playing than Jerome Callet. Anyone who'd like to dispute this needs to spend a few hours talking and playing with the gentleman, who is also a very gentle man, though the power in his trumpet playing is capable of tearing down more than just the walls of Jericho!

DANIEL J. PATRYLAK served as Solo Cornetist with The United States Marine Corps, *President's Own* Band. Dan also taught at Eastman (where he founded the Eastman Brass Quintet), the University of Texas (where he served as Dean of the School of Music), and the University of Connecticut (where he served as Department Chair and Trumpet Professor). Dan's exquisite technique and eloquent musicality combine to make him the teacher's teacher and the trumpeter's trumpet player. Though I had previously studied with both Vacchiano and Broiles, I learned more about trumpet technique and solo literature from Dan than either of those other greats. Dan's example of humanitarianism has also been a great source of inspiration to me. I continue to turn to Dan musically, as a teacher, and as a mentor in life. He has been a true friend to me in the best sense of the word for decades and I look forward to many more years of friendship and inspiration with him!

All that I have to offer comes from the roots given me by these wonderful teachers. My gratitude is un-ending, my appreciation eternal.

Teaching is the only profession that affects eternity.

CHAPTER 22

In Conclusion

The Journey Continues

This is where we part company for the time being. It's time for you to continue the trip on your own, to be your own best teacher.

Be your own best artist. That bears repeating:

BE YOUR OWN BEST ARTIST!

You have the roadmap, the side-trips, and the knowledge to maintain and develop your performance life. Now go and apply what you've learned!

I'll be here, on TPIN and Trumpet Herald, and approachable via email (jgpocius@yahoo.com) should you have questions you can't decipher on your own. You can always re-read this book, in whole or in part.

And you always have the option of coming to Boston for a personal CHOPCHECK™ with me.

But in the end you have to drive the horn yourself.

You can do it!

Believe in yourself and believe in the music.

God-speed and enjoy the trip!

APPENDIX I

Biography of Jeanne Gabriel Pocius

Trumpet Teacher and Performer Jeanne Gabriel Pocius was born in Manchester, Connecticut, the fourth of five children. Her mother had been a singer in big bands and her father had been a Marine Corps bugler in World War II, in the Pacific.

Jeanne began to play the trumpet at the age of seven, was playing professionally by the age of ten, and teaching adults by the age of 12. Her daily practice habits supplemented the weekly lessons in public school, given by itinerant music teachers Catherine Wade and Marty Goldstein.

Jeanne's ability on trumpet was recognized by a priest at her home church, St. Joseph's, in Willimantic, CT. Father Joseph Kugler would become a long-term mentor: introducing her to the piccolo trumpet repertoire and the recordings of the great Maurice Andre, the world's premier trumpet soloist.

In her early teens Jeanne began to experiment with jazz and was soon performing regularly with the Maurice Bergeron Dance Orchestra, a combo of experienced musicians, many of whom began playing jazz in the early part of the 20th century and were in their seventh or eighth decade at the time. Her fascination with traditional jazz continues to this day and was greatly buoyed by working with Bo, Bill and Ed Winiker, of the Winiker Swing Orchestras in Boston.

By the time she was a junior in high school Jeanne was playing with several professional groups, including symphony and pops orchestras, concert and jazz bands, and a brass ensemble as well as her high school's musical organizations.

In February of her senior year of high school, while studying with Robert Lemons of Eastern Connecticut University, Jeanne won the Bertha Plasse award and the opportunity to perform the Arutunian Trumpet Concerto with the Eastern Connecticut Symphony Orchestra, under the direction of Victor Norman.

Soon after, Jeanne auditioned for and was accepted as a student by William Vacchiano (Principal Trumpet of the New York Philharmonic Orchestra for 37 years).

Jeanne matriculated at the University of Connecticut, where Vacchiano was in residence. She later also studied with Mel Broiles (Principal Trumpet of the Metropolitan Opera Orchestra) and Daniel Patrylak (Founder of Eastman Brass Quintet and Solo Cornetist with the *President's Own* United States Marine Corps Band).

While in undergraduate study, Jeanne sought out every opportunity to perform, including marching, concert and chamber ensembles, experimental and traditional theater orchestras, and jazz, rock and reggae bands.

Following the birth of her son, she continued her studies on a part-time basis while both working and performing.

In post-graduate study and master classes, Jeanne worked with Rolf Smedvig, Walter Chesnut, Jeffrey Holmes, Charles Treger, Elizabeth Green, H. Robert Reynolds, Gene Young, Paul Lavalle, and Jerome Callet.

Jeanne currently lives, teaches and freelances in the greater Boston, Massachusetts, area of the United States. She has performed in classical and jazz venues throughout the Eastern United States, Western Europe, Eastern Canada, and the Caribbean.

Jeanne's professional credits include principal trumpet positions in the Cape Ann Symphony, Charles Peckham's American Musical Theater, the Manchester Symphony and Pops, the Hillyer Festival Orchestra, the Harvard Musical Association Orchestra, the Erevan Orchestra and Choral Society, the Eastern Connecticut Symphony, the North Shore Philharmonic, and numerous musical theater organizations and smaller ensembles, both jazz and classical, throughout the greater New England area.

She has performed as lead trumpet for the Winiker Orchestras, the Tom Roli Big Band, the Dave Rasmussen Big Band, the Jan Garber Band, the Gene Krupa Band, the Swing Out Big Band, the Anguilla Jazz Ensemble (*AJE*), the Moonglow Big Band, and many name acts, including Aretha Franklin, the Temptations, Bob Hope, Phyllis Diller, Joan Rivers, the Beatty-Cole Circus, Skitch Henderson, Roberta Peters, George Shearing, and Sergio Franchi.

Jeanne has served as trumpet instructor for Gordon College, Salem State College, St. John's Preparatory School, Philips Exeter Academy, the University of Connecticut, the University of Massachusetts at Amherst, and various school systems through Massachusetts and Connecticut.

She has in-person and cyber-students living on six continents that correspond with her via email, telephone, and SKYPE and fly into Boston for their periodic CHOPCHECK^{TM}.

Jeanne can be heard regularly performing as part of the jazz duo, *Password*, with guitarist Hank Wiktorowicz. She also has a swing combo (*Sophisticated Swing*), a big band (*Moonglow*), and a brass quintet (the *North Shore Brass*). She also maintains a busy solo performance schedule, performing for wedding ceremonies and recitals in the greater Boston area and the Caribbean.

APPENDIX II

Selected writings for TPIN*
Trumpet Players International Network

The Trumpet Players' International Network is an internet list serv, established in 1993 by Dr. Michael Anderson, trumpet professor at Dana College at the time. Thousands of trumpet professionals, students, amateurs and "comeback players" (trumpeters who played earlier in life, took a sabbatical from playing and are now returning to playing again) interact through TPIN on a daily basis through an email interface. The following are samples of Jeanne Pocius' postings to TPIN over the years.

I. A Philosophy of Teaching

Sadly there is still much misinformation about the playing musical instruments. Much of that is perpetuated by those who continue to teach *what works for me*, when the truth is as obvious as to be ignored, that truth being:

What works for YOU is what your teacher needs to emphasize!

Think of how many students were misled by the *smile system* school of thought, then by the *frown* system (which is, after all, merely a *smile* turned upside down), and lately by the *Tighten your corners* school, which is, once again, a reincarnation of the *smile system* in new wrapping paper.

The truth is that any system will work, TO A POINT!!! The facts are that any system that works against your natural setup will inhibit you at some point. Those who have switched from trombone or baritone or flute to trumpet will need to use tighter corners for a while, until they develop better small motor control of the orbicularis oris muscle. (That muscle is much more lax in those types of players, including the tubists, who rely so much on *song and wind* that they sometimes forget the necessity of using the smaller muscles to support the air.)

Think of this: If, when you were learning to write, the teacher insisted that you hold the pencil in a way that was difficult or impossible for you; would you have learned to write very well? No, of course not! Or, if the teacher told you to concentrate on what you wanted to write, not the process of writing, would you then be able to maneuver the pencil, without knowing how to form the letters? Again, of course not. Or even, if the teacher told you to concentrate on the muscles of your arm or the *flow of the paper across your desk* could you then write?

No. You needed first to learn to hold the pencil (which required you and/or your teacher being able to recognize which hand was dominant, or you'd be fighting the whole time for mastery of an alien hand), then to apply the pencil to paper, at first using a large, thick pencil and writing in huge letters, then (as you gained mastery) learning to use smaller size pencil and print. Finally you learned to write in cursive, with a fine-line pen or even a fountain pen, or perhaps even mastering the fine art of calligraphy!

In playing any instrument much the same process must be followed. Sometimes we must regress to the point of holding the pencil (locating the mouthpiece on the lips, or even correcting the size of the mouthpiece).

Sometimes, we need only go over the formation of certain letters, or change the angle (left to right) or tilt (pivot: up or down) of the paper (instrument).

But it is always far easier to teach the right way from the beginning than it is to undertake remedial work.

That is why I advocate using the very low pedals, even from the first lesson for beginners. That is also why I feel buzzing to be important. There are those who can play without buzzing first, but their row becomes much harder to hoe without removing those big rocks (non-buzzing styles of playing) first.

It is important, always to move from mastering larger muscles (and concepts) to smaller ones (like learning general principles in school before specializing in a particular field).

The slow, low pedals enable good buzzing. I DON'T advocate the first octave of pedals. Why? Because they inevitably lead to bad habits in beginners or CP (comeback players), such as closed teeth and open apertures (both are bad things).

Once someone has become advanced, and their embouchure is strong and stable almost ANY exercise can be applied beneficially. But I feel it is irresponsible to advocate such exercises for less than advanced players.

Too often, again, there are players who are very strong, who advocate what works best for THEM, not for the student who is seeking guidance.

That's why I strive to understand the student, and offer general principles first, before the specifics and the details of development.

Beyond the buzzing of lips and mouthpiece, and the use of the double-low pedals (*elepharts* or *elephant farts* as we kiddingly call them), I like to use lip trills (at first just one note to one other note, then later the actual trills or shakes), and flexibilities. (Even with young players, I encourage them to do lip trills on their mouthpieces, imitating a bee, a lawnmower, or a siren--police or fire in the US, I don't know if that works worldwide, though).

And tonguing is very important. I begin the q syllable early on as well. Always emphasizing the shape of the tongue in articulations as well as the striking surface.

And most important of all is the use of the **eternal airstream**. Keep the energy flowing even after you cease to produce a sound. This is a key to musicality in performance.

II. A Philosophy of Music

(From interview with Ole J Utnes, "The Chop Doc Speaks")

It probably sounds hokey to say so, but music is such an integral part of my life. I have a real passion for it. And I hear it everywhere: not just in organized sounds, but in the sounds of wind, rain, even the quiet peacefulness of snow has its own music.

Do you know that even those who are severely hearing-impaired (we used to say *deaf*) are capable of participating in music (I recall a particular bass player, whose name I sadly can't remember, who is deaf and learned to play by feeling the vibrations of the bass through the instrument.) Of course, with the advent of electronic tuners this becomes even more plausible.

Very few people are truly *tone-deaf.* Many who thought they were merely haven't had a teacher take the time to teach them how to regard music.

I have an excellent student on the trumpet who is a professional ski instructor. He'll often translate my analogies in skiing analogies to help himself better understand.

Well, I am probably the most *ski-deaf* or *ski-blind* person you could imagine. I've only just begun to learn to roller-blade (a dangerous task at my age!), and the concept of speeding down a snowy incline with only a couple of twigs in your hands, and a couple of thin slabs of wood on your feet is VERY frightening to me.

And yet (Elie Wiesel uses that expression a great deal in his autobiography), I believe that my student has helped me to better understand skiing with his analogies, and that, perhaps, some day I may even attempt to ski (cross-country, though, I think, I'm not brave enough to try downhill<!>).

So, if we look and listen for music in all that we do, it only enhances our musical performances. The greatest artists are those who approach the *Renaissance man* ideal of studying and understanding all of the arts and sciences (in which I include mathematics, which so many musicians tend to have a natural ability for studying).

The more diverse your background, the more interesting your musical interpretations will be for all kinds of performances.

Bach's "SDG" - can you relate to that?

Soli Deo Gloria. All give glory to God or *To God be all glory.*

Each of my performances, every composition, lyric, orchestration, in fact, each day of my life is offered in praise and thanksgiving to the great God who has given us the magnificent gifts of life and music.

My own expression is: *To Thee, o Lord, with gladness, to the glory of God!* But it's the same sentiment: that of *giving back the gift* by developing and sharing it.

Talents are wasted when not used, and are best used by sharing. You may be the greatest trumpeter in the world in the practice room, able to single tongue sixteenth notes at quarter note=400, or the like, but if you're not sharing your abilities with others, then you're not expressing gratitude to the Lord for the gifts given you.

I don't care if all you can play is a few simple songs. Go out and play for someone else! There are senior citizens, veterans in hospitals, invalids, shut-ins, homeless folks. Go out and play for them. Play for your church, temple, or fellowship group. Play for children, play for family, for neighbors, for friends. It doesn't matter for whom you play as long as you are playing, and to the very best of your ability each time you do so.

A side stream benefit of this is that, with so much performing under your belt, you'll seldom, if ever, suffer from stage fright--performing becomes second nature to you.

Remember that music is a social art, and a gracious gift from God. Return that gift every chance you get and it will grow (and exponentially so!).

To THEE, o Lord, with gladness. To the Glory of GOD!

III. Performance Anxiety

Performance anxiety is a vestigial remnant of our caveman heritage. Better known as the "flight or fight syndrome," it's our body and mind's response to real or perceived danger/stress.

Often the perceived stress or danger (such as occurs in performance anxiety) is more difficult to manage than actual danger (which can be walked away from) because our "rational" mind attempts to belittle the very real, physiological response that has been triggered at an instinctive level.

There is no easy answer. I wish I could give you one. But really the only way I've found to alleviate this situation is to begin talking about the fun and excitement of performance from the very first lesson I have with young players. I keep building upon that attitude so that the kids develop a sense of thrill and excitement rather than fear and anxiety (really two sides of the same coin, it becomes a matter of regard, rather than awareness.)

You see the response is the same whether you're walking out on stage to perform, or standing in line waiting to go for a ride on that new roller coaster, or waiting for your first date with someone new.

Think about it: the butterflies in the stomach, the dry mouth, the upset stomach, the shaking and/or sweaty palms, and the tensed jaw (leading in extreme to a pseudo-lockjaw effect).

Different stimuli, but the same responses.

How to deal with it?

Well, there are several different approaches that work to varying degrees. A lot depends on your overall response to stress.

For some folks, deep breathing (so called "Yogic cleansing breaths", in which you breathe in deeply through the nose, and exhale through slightly compressed lips with the air slightly pressurized, all the while visualizing the tension flowing out of your body) is sufficient.

For some, a sort of self-hypnosis and imaging technique is helpful (wherein you visualize yourself, confident, successful, happy, and confident, performing the entire performance with great joy and proficiency).

For some, having a high-complex-carbohydrate meal (but low in bulk, to avoid discomfort when using torso muscles) will provide the needed confidence and energy.

For some, a dietary supplement of "Stress-tabs" (vitamin B complex plus vitamin C) will prove calming enough.

For some, herbal supplement (such as "Kava-Kava" or "Valerian") will assist in calming them.

For some, merely recognizing that they are "keyed up" rather than "nervous" will make the difference.

And for some, medical or pharmaceutical treatment is the only recourse.

With all of the above approaches, I think nothing succeeds quite so much as finding a place where you can successfully perform without feeling stressed (catch yourself 'doing it right" and build on that success). Maybe that would consist of playing for senior citizens, or for your local church, or even for your cats. (And I'm not being facetious--any external, non-judgmental audience will do--the key is to rediscover the joy of performing.)

Finally, and this is one of the most difficult things I can say on the subject, there may be some for whom performance is not an option.

Practicing, and playing with recordings and/or software (like "Vivace" or "Band-In-A-Box") may be a viable alternative for those for whom public performance is detrimental to your health.

Personally, I'm an optimist who likes to believe that no obstacle is insurmountable (think of Philippians, for those of you who read Scripture), given the correct approach, but finding that approach can take a great deal of time and effort.

Sometimes, you also need to know that a missed note here or there is not the end of the world. Professionals recognize that a performance needn't be "note-perfect" to be a success.

Give yourself some room to make mistakes, otherwise how are you going to learn from them?

Best advice: remember why you love to play, and share that love with your audience (I remember one master class, years ago, now, when the artist told us to project feelings of love toward the audience and our colleagues before walking out on stage. It's been many years and I don't remember her name, but the image and technique have stayed with me-- and worked<!> for many performances.)

We all feel the same feelings before performing; the key is to focus those feelings into a peak performance, rather than allowing them to devolve into generalized fear.

IV.   Post about "TAPS"

(From interview with Ole J Utnes, "The Chop Doc Speaks")

In U.S. you often use the trumpet (bugle) in a funeral (Jeannie, I'm thinking of your beautiful post about that)

Yes, TAPS is the final tribute to veterans in our country. The piece was written on the battlefield (or in camp after a battle) during our country's civil war in the latter part of the 19th century.

Let me share a post I sent to TPIN about TAPS with you:

Dear Jim:

I'm sure we've all had experiences like yours with playing Taps for the funerals of friends and family members.

Remember that it's a service to the mourners for them to release their tears. Unspent grief is acid to the soul, and manifests itself in strange ways.

I've often been told by funeral directors that family members had remained absolutely stoic during visiting hours, religious services, and even graveside services, but finally let go when the trumpeter sounded Taps (sometimes it doesn't happen 'til the echo, which I usually play facing the opposite direction, and usually try for an actual acoustic echo as well.)

I've been blessed with four fathers in my life: my biological Dad, a dear friend who was a priest, my college director of bands, and a beloved colleague/band leader with whom I performed for many years.

The reason I share this with you is that, over the last three years, I have lost all of them, and performed at each funeral. I can tell you that, while it never gets any easier to play for someone that you loved, the discipline of practice and performance can carry you through when your heart fails you.

For the first, my beloved friend and mentor, Fr. Joseph Kugler, I played "La Grace" and the "Concerto in D" (yes, the one that soars on the first movement) by Telemann, then played "Hyfrydol" and "Amazing Grace" at the graveside.

For my own father, Felix Peter Pocius, who had been a Marine Corps bugler in WWII, I played the entire Mass, including an original arrangement of the largo movement from the "New World Symphony" in a duet with John Archer (who is a basso vocalist), Taps, and "A Trumpeter's Lullaby" for the exit music.

For Edward Winiker (the long term bandleader, and founder of the Winiker Orchestras of Boston/Washington DC/and Florida), I played "Trumpeter's Lullaby" a capella at the very foot of his grave, with the family standing nearby, and dozens of musical colleagues surrounding us.

And finally, most recently, I played for Allan Gillespie, the Director of Bands Emeritus of the University of Connecticut, for whom I played, at the widow's request, "Prayer of St. Gregory." I stood, alone, at the front of the church, facing the family, with the organ/accompanist in the back of the church, in the choir loft, which made the organ interlude, between the second and final trumpet entrances seem absolutely eternal (I was nearly sobbing after making the mistake of looking directly at the family members.)

But, thankfully, once the mouthpiece touched my lips, something else took over (an auto-pilot, as it were) and I was able to complete the task, faithful to the memory of a fine conductor and trumpet player in his own right.

The point of this is to encourage all of you to have the strength to share your gift with others--It can be very healing, for them as well as for you yourself, to share that which is inexpressible in any other way through the beautiful sound of the trumpet.

I thank God for the gifts of music.

V. Why Choose the Trumpet?

Answer:

1. Because no other instrument sounds like a trumpet.

2. Because no other instrument _feels_ like a trumpet.

3. Because no other instrument makes you feel like you're singing like a trumpet does.

4. Because no other instrument gets to play the same variety of musical styles in the same way as the trumpet.

5. Because no other instrument can boast of also enamoring: Harry James, Louis Armstrong, Mannie Klein, Rafael Mendez, Maurice Andre, Roy Eldridge, Cootie Williams, Ziggy Elman, Bunny Berigan, Billy Butterfield, Bill Vacchiano, Mel Broiles, Phil Smith, Tom Stevens, Bill Adams, Clyde Hunt, Michael Anderson, Bud Herseth, Mundy Ghitalla, Timofey Dokshizer, Ian McKechnie, Greg Alley, Al Lilly, Eddie Lewis, Jeff Parke, John Lynch, Rich Szabo, Roger Voisin, Nick Mondello, you, and me!

6. Because no other instrument gets to enjoy TPIN quite the way we do. ;^)

7. Because you love it more than you've ever loved anyone or anything else, even though it sometimes seems like you hate it almost as much!

8. Because only a trumpet player could get away with dressing like Doc does without being labeled with deleterious terminology <G>.

9. Because no other instrument lets you blow off steam quite so well. ;^)

And finally:

10. Because you don't choose the trumpet--The trumpet chooses YOU!

VI. Interpretation of Arutunian Trumpet Concerto

Aleksander Arutiunian is, indeed, Armenian, and his brilliant trumpet concerto should be approached as though telling the story of the brave Armenian people.

For those of you who do not know the story: the majority of the Armenian population was massacred early in the 20th century in a genocide which reportedly gave Hitler the idea that "No one cared about the Armenians, why should they care about the Jews?" (Not my view, but a reported quote from Hitler in justification of his "final solution").

The opening fanfare can be viewed as a story-teller grabbing the attention of the audience, and preparing to set the stage for the saga to come. It should be played in a bravura style, somewhat ad libitum in tempo, with huge dynamic contrasts.

A (ALLEGRO ENERGICO)

At the opening statement of the march, you should present it as though you are singing a fighting song of the brave Armenian people. Listen to the music and you can hear hooves beating, swords clashing, and great valor, though there is also a sense of desperation in the running eighths and sixteenths at the top of the second page of the solo part (as published by International, which I will reference throughout this summary).

D (MENO MOSSO)

The next entrance is descriptive of the beautiful artwork of the Armenian peoples (the oriental rugs, the beautiful icons in the churches, the wonderfully lush and rich musical heritage), including a wonderful symbolic weaving of melody and counter-melody between the solo trumpeter and the orchestra..

G (TEMPO I)

This is broken into by the next section, which displays vignettes of horror as the massacre begins. There is even a short little bit of a lullaby as a grandmother, perhaps tries to soothe a child into silence to try to save its life--This is abruptly cut-off with a loud chop of a crescendo, leading to the near-scream of a final note for the trumpet in this section.

M (MENO MOSSO)

The next section, brought in by the sobbing rhythms of the accompaniment is a threnody for those lost in the genocide, even quoting a bit of the earlier mentioned lullaby, and weeping, weeping for those lost.

O (A TEMPO to end)

Finally, there is a gentle movement back toward the major and a dedication to make a difference in the world: that this should never be forgotten. The tale is once again begun, and the heroic march heard again until the final two-beat triplet and final note sound the cry: "NEV-ER FOR-GET!"

Bearing this description in mind, one can easily cut the cadenza, if necessary, and also make a cut after the threnody, leading into the final march. Perhaps the cello or piano player could as easily or even more easily cut the repeats in their classical era pieces. Besides, the Arutunian really only lasts about 20 minutes anyway and audiences **love** it -- it's so much more exciting than the usual concerto fare.

BTW, my first solo performance with a professional symphony orchestra was the Arutunian, performed from memory when I was a senior in high school and won a young artists' competition with it.

The Armenian information comes via the Erevan Choir and Orchestra, conducted by Father Oshagan Minassian (who is an Armenian Catholic priest), for which I have played principal trumpet for several years now.

Hope this has helped. And don't ever let anyone tell you that this concerto isn't beautiful music!

VII. On Loving the Trumpet

Dear Liz:

One statement in your post says it all: "My son loves the trumpet." Love is such a great motivator, that it, along with faith, is capable of moving mountains. It's not such a big leap to understand that it will be sufficient to allow a little boy to learn to play the instrument that he loves<!>.

A number of studies have demonstrated that the instrument whose sound is most appreciated by a student is the one at which he or she will eventually excel most. It sounds very much like your son's "teacher" (and I use that term advisedly, and only because you used it in describing the person to whom you'd been paying money to "teach" your son to play the instrument he loves) doesn't know much about teaching youngsters.

The first few years of playing any instrument can be frustrating--there are so many factors involved in becoming proficient, including physical, cognitive, technical, and artistic, that it takes a person who is really caring and patient to teach beginners.

It sounds like the person who has discouraged your son is neither patient nor caring.

In nearly 30 years of teaching I have found only two students I really could not teach. Both were developmentally delayed. One was truly "pitch-deaf" (could not distinguish the difference between any pitches/sounds), but eventually went on to participate as a percussionist in the junior high and senior high bands. The other spent an entire year without being able to control his body sufficiently to remember the difference between two notes.

In other words, he was able to produce the two notes physically, with help on fingering and singing of the notes, but could not reproduce them, even with a tape recorder and a tape of the lesson for reference in his practicing at home.

That youngster, now a young man, still runs to hug me and talk about his "trumpet lessons" (many years later, now), and share with me his delight at being a custodian for a local bagel shop. Even though he "couldn't" play the trumpet, he believed he did for that year, and it's left him with a sense of pride and joy in his accomplishment that I wouldn't want to take away from him, would you?

So, let your son play the trumpet. There are many compensating factors that can be learned, regardless of his current teeth/jaw/lip configuration, to help him in his journey of discovery.

And frankly, in my town there is a young man who suffers from a neuro-muscular disease--lives in a wheelchair, has the use of only one hand (and that is limited), and yet he plays trumpet in the high school band. Of course, he'll never play first chair, never achieve a "high C" (let alone a double or triple high C), but that doesn't matter.

He's a member of the band. He's part of a peer group of some of the finest kids in the school (the band members). He interacts daily with some outstanding educators who view challenges as a daily part of life to be lived with, not fought with or run away from.

Those teachers see progress in even the <u>attempt</u> to begin the journey, not just in achieving the destination (and no, before you ask, it's not the school at which I teach). And he brings such pure, unadulterated JOY to his celebration of life and music that I can't conceive of ANYone telling him he "can't ever play the trumpet" just because he's living with a life-threatening neuro-muscular disease.

He's too busy living that life to worry about such trivialities.

No, Liz, you keep your son playing that trumpet! Encourage him, even on the days when he hates it (and there will be some of those days as well, as there are in any love relationship, since love and hate tend to be two sides of the same coin of passion.) His life will be far richer and more beautiful, as will be the lives of all those who interact with him.

As far as that so-called "teacher": tell him or her to get in touch with TPIN (the trumpet players' international network) and Michael Anderson. That person needs to learn what real teaching is about--helping the student discover and develop their greatest human potential, not just ensuring that they will succeed on one particular instrument.

And stay in touch with us yourself, please, Liz, and let us know the details as your son continues his journey with his trumpet. We care! We've been where he is now, and we'll stick with him, whenever he needs us, every step along the way.

VIII. A Trumpeter's Twelve Days of Christmas

(Sung to the 12 days of Christmas)
(With nods to our colleagues on TPIN)

On the first day of Christmas, my teacher gave to me:
A GR Mouthpiece for Triple High C!

On the second day of Christmas, my teacher gave to me:
Two Bottles of Binak and a GR mouthpiece for triple high C!

On the third day of Christmas, my teacher gave to me:
Three New Year's Eve gigs, two bottles of Binak, and a GR mouthpiece for triple high C!

On the fourth day of Christmas, my teacher gave to me:
Four Shulman systems, three new year's eve gigs, two bottles of Binak and a GR mouthpiece for triple high C!

On the fifth day of Christmas, my teacher gave to me:
FIIIIIVE TASTEE BROS!
Four Shulman systems, three New Year's Eve gigs, two bottles of Binak, and a GR mouthpiece for triple high C!

On the sixth day of Christmas, my teacher gave to me:
Six Mike Vax cases, FIIIIIVE TASTEE BROS! Four Shulman systems, three New Year's Eve gigs, two bottles of Binak, and a GR mouthpiece for triple high C!

On the seventh day of Christmas, my teacher gave to me:
Seven slots on youtube, Six Mike Vax cases, FIIIIIVE
TASTEE BROS! Four Shulman systems, three New Year's
Eve gigs, two bottles of Binak, and a GR mouthpiece for
triple high C!

On the eighth day of Christmas, my teacher gave to me:
Eight Bop Duets, Seven slots on youtube, Six Mike Vax
cases, FIIIIIVE TASTEE BROS! Four Shulman systems,
three New Year's Eve gigs, two bottles of Binak, and a GR
mouthpiece for triple high C!

On the ninth day of Christmas, my teacher gave to me:
Nine tubes of Zaja, eight Bop Duets, Seven slots on
youtube, Six Mike Vax cases, FIIIIIVE TASTEE BROS!
Four Shulman systems, three New Year's Eve gigs, two
bottles of Binak, and a GR mouthpiece for triple high C!

On the tenth day of Christmas, my teacher gave to me:
Ten Chase Sanborn CDs, Nine tubes of Zaja, eight Bop
Duets, Seven slots on youtube, Six Mike Vax cases,
FIIIIIVE TASTEE BROS! Four Shulman systems, three
New Year's Eve gigs, two bottles of Binak, and a GR
mouthpiece for triple high C!

On the eleventh day of Christmas, my teacher gave to me:
Eleven bids on Ebay, Ten Chase Sanborn CDs, Nine tubes
of Zaja, eight Bop Duets, Seven slots on youtube, Six Mike
Vax cases, FIIIIIVE TASTEE BROS! Four Shulman
systems, three New Year's Eve gigs, two bottles of Binak,
and a GR mouthpiece for triple high C!

On the twelfth day of Christmas, my teacher gave to me: Twelve Hickman text books, Eleven bids on Ebay, Ten Chase Sanborn CDs, Nine tubes of Zaja, eight Bop Duets, Seven slots on youtube, Six Mike Vax cases, FIIIIVE TASTEE BROS! Four Shulman systems, three New Year's Eve gigs, two bottles of Binak, and a GR mouthpiece for triple high C!

IX. "Music"

Of course, "MUSIC" is what this is all about. Any pedagogist will tell you that the end is what necessitates the means.

If trumpeters were all completely intuitive, then the "think" system, as so avidly practiced by the mythical Professor Harold Hill, would be the only system necessary to be able to play like Roy Eldridge, Dizzy Gillespie, Timofey Dokshitzer, Maurice Andre, etc.

But reality, unfortunately, intrudes. The reason I've had to analyze is that I've had students who weren't able to "make the connection" between what they've heard and what they needed or wanted to produce.

Thankfully, I've also had pupils who were blessed with the ability to play nearly anything once they'd heard it, but I can't say that they were typical.

Personally, I try to make a point of listening, not only to other trumpeters, but to many different types of musicians and music, and have played everything from symphonic to reggae.

If I've erred on the level of over-analysis for those of the members of this list who are capable of achieving results without others' advice and experience, mea culpa, but the responses I've received tend to show the converse to be true. Many of the members of this list are "amateurs"(consider the root of that word, which is "to love"--not a bad place to start) and appreciate hearing about different ways to explain the phenomena of trumpet playing or embouchure or what have you.

The bottom line is that we're all in this for the music, and anything we do, say, think, feel, or anything we choose to play on, be it a particular horn, mouthpiece, mute or whatever is merely a tool to assist us in expressing the music which lives in our hearts and souls and begs for the release of performance.

X. Some Advice to Young Students

(From interview with Ole J Utnes, "The Chop Doc Speaks")

Listen, listen, LISTEN! Listen to great musicians of EVERY ilk -- NOT just trumpet players, but great singers, great pianists, whatever. You'll be amazed at what you'll learn: how you'll learn to phrase and ornament more creatively because you've developed a greater aural palette.

Practice constantly, even away from the horn (This means "isometric" exercises and horseflaps). Whistle, too, it helps to develop your orbicularis oris muscles. Think in solfege syllables (it will help your soloing, improvising and sight-reading).

Find a great teacher, and learn all you can from them, and then find another, and another. They don't always have to be teachers for you to learn from them, either -- I learn something from every trumpeter I meet, no matter how young or inexperienced they might be -- They still have unique insights that might at some point become beneficial to me or another student.

Stay fit and healthy. Eat and drink well, but wisely. No one deserves to develop nutritionally related illnesses, and in the long run, I think, perhaps, all illnesses have their roots in poor nutrition.

Exercise your body and your mind and your spirit. Stasis is the worst habit you can develop, whether it is physical, intellectual, or spiritual.

Cultivate a spiritual awareness: acknowledge that your talent is a gift from God, and do your best to develop it and share it, since that is always the best way to give thanks for the gift of talent.

Play every chance you get, regardless of the circumstances, and (at least in the earlier stages of life) whether or not you get compensated for your efforts. Try to gain experience in many different styles, it will help you to be a more-rounded player in whatever style you eventually choose to call home (or even freelancing, which is what I truly enjoy the most).

Study and cultivate beauty wherever it exists, remembering that every drop of beauty you help to create or preserve enables future generations to build upon a foundation of goodness and accomplishment, rather than evil and destructiveness.

Seek to always expand the palettes of your life, be they musical, technique, knowledge, history, or whatever. The more interesting you are as a person, the more mature you will be as an artist.

Finally, don't forget why you started to play in the first place (because you LOVED the sound of the trumpet). Even when you are angry with yourself or your instrument (and it happens to all of us sooner or later in the practice/performance game), never put it down.

The great Daniel Patrylak (founder of the Eastman Brass Quintet, Solo Cornetist with the USMC's President's Own Marine Corps Band, and one of the finest musician-teachers it has been my honor to know) once told me in a particularly frustrating (for me) lesson (when I had put the trumpet down on the table and said "That's it! I just CAN't play it!"): (said in a very firm, but EXTREMELY quiet voice) "Pick that trumpet up! Don't you ever put it down again! That's not the way I want you to behave and that's not the way you're GOING to behave!"

Needless to say, the horn hasn't ever been put back down since!

One final thought I would wish you to carry with you:

There is always music, my friends, even when there is no light, no warmth, and no food. There is always music.

In the words of Star Trek, the Next Generation's Captain Jean-Luc Picard:

Make it so!

XI. Challenges

I want to address a factor that has been raised several times in this thread, though not quite as directly as I hope to address it.

That factor is "challenge," its nature and the performer's response to same.

In my "practice" as a trumpet teacher (well into my fourth decade as a teacher), I've had numerous students who faced challenges in their trumpet playing.

Some were simply (though not to them) facing a poorly set-up embouchure, which caused a variety of additional issues, including performance anxieties based on past, poor performances due to their less-than-efficient physical set-up.

Some were dealing with poor equipment (by far the easiest problem to remedy, especially these days, with so many excellent trumpets and mouthpieces available to purchase).

Some were dealing with physical issues (a past tracheotomy, trauma to lips, facial nerves, teeth, limbs, lungs, tongue, Bell's palsy, diabetes, blood pressure and/or diabetic issues, Parkinson's disease, cancer in various stages of treatment/remission/relapse).

Some were dealing with mental health issues (anxiety itself, mental illness, addiction illness, mental retardation, autism, psychosis, depression.)

In each case, I've viewed my job as a teacher as that of empowering the particular student to realize their best abilities. This is without losing my own perspective of reality, nor losing my wonder and delight at the miracles which can occur for students who truly love what they are doing and are capable of "making the connection" between that love and these jealous muses of trumpet playing and music.

When I was a younger teacher, I expected every student to work as hard as I had during my younger years. My junior high school students were told to practice 3 hours per day, or "suffer the wrath of Jeanne", and many left unsuccessful lessons in tears. And I thought I was a successful teacher because most of those students went on to play professionally.

Now, thankfully, I have gained a deeper, more valid perspective as a teacher, and recognize that each student has his or her own path to follow, goal to achieve, voice to be heard.

Sometimes that voice is one that will only be heard in private practice, or communion with their Creator.

Sometimes it is a voice that will be shared with many.

Sometimes it will meet my personal definition of successful performance, sometimes it will meet _their_ personal definition of success (which may be completely the opposite of a professional performer's idea of success).

Many of you know that a few years ago I accepted a job running an elementary band program for a local public school system.

This was something I had eschewed for most of the years of my professional life, preferring to be a private and /or college teacher to the corporate world of public school.

Last night, my youngsters in this year's beginning band program had their first formal concert for the year.

We had had two full-scale dress rehearsals, respectfully one and two weeks prior to the concert (though not in the concert location), but were only able to access the auditorium 90 minutes before the scheduled performance, due to the 3 snow days this week.

I welcome a high percentage of challenged children into my program, including behaviorally, emotionally, and physically challenged students.

Last night I witnessed a miracle occurring: In one of my individual school bands (there are six different school bands in the program, plus the combined, all-city band, and I conduct all band rehearsals and concerts, plus teaching all the lessons from flutes to "nuts", which are, of course, percussionists!), there are <u>nine</u> "SPED" students, including one severely DD (Developmentally delayed---used to be called mentally retarded), several autistic of varying degrees, and one boy, "G", who is multi-challenged (wears two hearing aids, very thick lensed glasses, is developmentally delayed, and has cerebral palsy, so is very challenged by simply walking and climbing up and down stairs.

It is "G" who performed the miracle last night.

In the course of the "dress rehearsal" before the concert and the concert itself, the children were required to walk on and off stage several times (this entailed climbing a set of several stairs from the audience to the stage).

As "G's" band entered and exited the stage, the entire group of band members and audience members were witnesses. This chubby, challenged boy, in meticulously correct concert attire of a white dress shirt, with long tie, black dress pants and shiny black shoes, was <u>very</u> slowly negotiating walking down and up the incline of the audience, up and down and up the stairs, into his proper seat, both for his individual band performance, and for the all-city performance.

He properly performed the commands for "concert rest position", "instruments up", attacked on the downbeat, released on the cut-off, played in time with his "neuro-typical" colleagues, bowed appropriately on cue, and most importantly of all: knew that he had done a good job and took pride in his efforts.

Believe me, mine were not the only tear-filled eyes in the hall.

Was "G" the best performer on stage, musically?

No, of course not, at least not from the standpoint of the teacher I was 25 or 30 years ago.

But his performance was a miracle and a success because no one told him it was "impossible" to perform with hearing, sighted, physically perfect, "Normal" kids.

And because he <u>LOVES</u> music, and loves being a part of "Band".

Twenty or thirty years ago, "G" would never have experienced the opportunity to play an instrument, be in band, and perform in a concert.

He may never do so again after this first year.

But for at least one year, he knows the delight of hearing an audience applaud for him and him alone (as we each experience in performance, if we are part of a larger ensemble or performing as a soloist, the effect is the same), and he will carry that experience with him throughout his entire life.

And I am <u>so</u> <u>privileged</u> to have been witness to his great triumph.

Some days it is so <u>humbling</u> to experience the calling of being a teacher.

XII. **What Is Success?**

You bring up an interesting point:

What IS "Success"?

To some it can only mean obtaining a principal trumpet position in a major symphony orchestra.

To others it might mean drawing enough breath to be able to play a single song for a loved one.

To some it might mean having the endurance to play several gigs in a single day without losing your chops.

To others it might mean finally gaining a third cornet chair in the local community band.

Might I suggest that, more than ability or effort or talent, "SUCCESS" is a matter of perspective?

Are you succeeding if others are impressed by your playing? (Even if you know you are not working to the level of your potential?) Are you succeeding if you can impress the guys in a local rehearsal band, but your chops are not reliable enough to get you that gig you've always wanted playing in the local community band/symphony? Are you succeeding if all you do is pick up the horn once per week to play with your church choir?

Maybe yes, maybe no.

It's all a matter of perspective, isn't it?

Let me give you an example: For many years, I allowed myself to coast as a player, playing enough to maintain my chops (in rehearsals, gigs, and lessons), but not really challenging myself unless I had a solo appearance or recital to give.

Was I succeeding?

To others, perhaps, but I had started to accept that I didn't need to strive any more (a dangerous, slippery slope!)

Then along came my beloved Terry, and suddenly it is not enough for me to coast: I want to be everything that God has challenged me to become: the best teacher, the best trumpet player, and the best person I could possibly be!

I've come to realize that part of my problem was an underlying depression and dis-satisfaction with the physical limitations various illness and challenges had placed in my way.

In other words: I'd begun to give up!

Yes, ME, the chop doc, who spends hours and hours pushing, challenging, encouraging and cajoling other trumpeters to be the best they can be, was failing to "heal myself".

Sobering thought.

I've come to realize, over the last six weeks, that many of the areas in which I'd thought I could not progress again are starting to grow. Even my triple tonguing, which had suffered from the throat surgery I underwent 4 1/2 years ago, when they removed the center of the hyoid bone from the base of my tongue, is starting to creep back upwards on the metronome!

It was my own ATTITUDE, my own PERSPECTIVE that was out-of-focus! I've seen this same sort of thing with some of my more-challenged students in the public schools: they had been labeled for SO long that they'd begun to believe that they could NOT achieve anything.

So they gave up trying.

Did I let them give up?

Nope.

I found SOMEthing at which they could succeed, and gradually, ever-so-carefully helped them to build upon that success to reach another small success, and then another slightly larger success, etc.

Would any of them become professional musicians? Highly unlikely, but each of them has achieved a new sense of self-awareness, self-esteem, pride.

And each is more ready to try to tackle a new challenge that comes along, which wouldn't have been likely before their musical encounters.

I guess the point I'm hoping to make here is that ANY of us can become discouraged and give in to the pookah on our shoulder who tries to poke us into complacency!

Don't give in! Don't give up!

You don't have to be Tim Morison, Phil Smith, or Chris Martin or Arturo Sandoval! Be Paddy or Warren or James or Jami or Michael or Tim or Pam or Nick or Marty.

But be the VERY best YOU can be:

Sometimes you'll be ready to meet the challenge, sometimes you won't.

Some days you'll have trouble taking the horn out of the case: but DO it, even if all you do are a few pedal tones and a couple of lip slurs.

The first step is ALways the hardest, you know!

And some days, you find it within yourself to accomplish GREAT things: You'll play that hymn or standard you've always wanted to do well: share it with the little old lady down the street or the folks in the nursing home across town (it will amplify your joy and theirs!).

Or you'll perform the Michael Haydn AND Brandenburg No. 2 in the same evening and NAIL them both!! (Yup, doing that again now!) I've heard it said that "G-d appreciates best the little things that are done with great care!" You can DO it!! And, these days, so can I!

XIII. Regarding Rants Against Non-Professional Players

I certainly sympathize with you, since I also have to play with players who don't always "meet the mark", let alone exceed it.

But, I am NOT an elitist about music or any other area of life.

(At least at this stage of my life---I do confess to being much less tactful, considerate, and accepting when I was a younger player struggling to make my mark as a player and being repeatedly frustrated by the politics of "who you know" rather than "how you play").

This, after all, is America, and the same freedom that allows us to vote for the candidates of our choice (at least in most elections) and work the jobs we choose, and live where we please, also allows amateurs to coexist with professionals in most walks of life.

There are, of course, those who virtually practice law, medicine and dentistry without licenses (we call them grandparents, parents, aunts, uncles, faith healers, ministers, etc).

And there are those who practice the arts, without benefit of training or experience or talent.

I believe firmly in the need to have the arts in education, and to have non-professionals and amateurs working with professionals.

When I was young, there were old-timers who took me under their wing and didn't care that I was brash, cocky and over-sure of myself (and, Chris, I PLAYED and practiced between 8-18 hours PER DAY when I was younger!), and taught me the ropes.

They did this before AND after I got my union card. And I continued to play with them long after they'd lost their edge as players, and learned to respect their musicality, even if their technical facility and edge had worn down.

Professional musicians don't have an exclusive right to perform, nor do they have the only messages to give.

God gives music to ALL of us, child, adult, amateur, professional, artist, virtuoso or hack---We all have something to give, something to say.

If this were an ideal place in which to live, artists of every type would be the best-paid, followed by teachers of all types, with politicians at the very BOTTOM of the barrel!

But it's not an ideal world, and the cultivation of TOLERANCE, in every way, shape and form, is what inevitably proffers peace and harmony, and not just in music!

Chris, by ALL means, continue to hone your skills and abilities.

But don't neglect to listen to those folks you're putting down---you might just learn something worth knowing in the process!

We need to count our blessings in being healthy, practicing trumpeters.

May we each both teach and learn on a daily basis,

Blessings,
Jeanne

APPENDIX III
Trumpeting, By Nature by Jeanne G Pocius
Daily Diagnostic CHOPCHECKtm

I. PREPARATORY EXERCISES/DEEP BREATHING
   A. Breathe deeply IN through your nose for a count of 7-9 seconds, and OUT through your mouth for a count of 11-13 seconds.

   B. Repeat breathing, but this time SIGH the air OUT with abdominal support.

   C. Repeat breathing, but this time purse your lips as you SIGH the air OUT.

II. BUZZING
   A. Wet lips, and blow air gently through lightly closed lips to produce a loose, flapping buzz.

   B. Wet lips and draw slightly toward center of lips before closing and buzzing to produce a stronger buzz with a pitch close to A 220 (the A below middle C).

   C. Apply mouthpiece to ANCHOR SPOTtm, and buzz pitched notes as notated below (Slurred):

III. PEDAL TONES (Double-low, "Elephant Farts")
   Play these very gently, starting two octaves below low C. Use full air for each

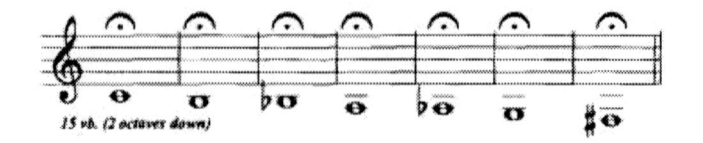

15 vb. (2 octaves down)

Copyright 2004, Jeanne G Pocius
All Rights Reserved

Daily Diagnostic CHOPCHECKtm, cont.

IV. Lip TONERS: (Play each by drawing lips slightly toward center, then slightly "pinching" lips together to achieve the interval jump. You should sense a "click" between the notes

A.

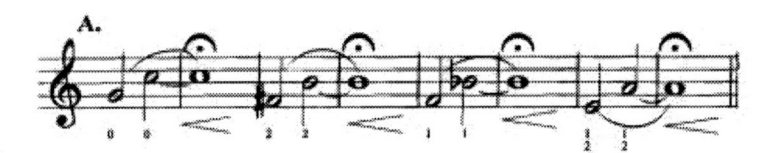

If at any time you fail to achieve the "click" between notes, or have trouble getting a note to speak, return to and repeat the pedal tones sequence.

B.

Focus on more of a centering of your lips, rather than compressing/pinching the lips together for maximum efficiency when playing the toners.

C.

Daily Diagnostic CHOPCHECKtm, cont.

V. TONGUING (Eyeblinkers): Play these VERY crisply, with a strong attack and a breath release. Set the tip of the tongue against the inside of the bottom lip. Allow breath pressure to build behind the tongue briefly by keeping the lips closed and the tongue set. Be careful to keep throat open and tongue forward. Release the tongue (drop onto top of bottom teeth) to release/attack the note.
When played properly, these often cause listeners to Blink, hence the nickname.

Play each repeat once to begin. Later increase each repeated section for many repetitions, and repeat the entire exercise several times to build strength.

A.

When you can comfortably play this open, repeat with all 2nd, all 1st, and all 1 & 2.

B.

When you can comfortably play this open, repeat with all 2nd, all 1st, and all 1 & 2.

Daily Diagnostic CHOPCHECKtm, cont.

For the following lines, play each all 1&2 fingerings, then all 1, all 2, and finally all Open.

You may continue these on successively higher harmonics, as desired.

Daily Diagnostic CHOPCHECKtm, cont.

VI. **RIPPLES:** These are fast, lazy octave slurs in which you want to hit every partial to create an effect like water rippling over rocks in a stream. Repeat each fingering for at least three repetitions, then move upward chromatically through the six fingering positions (13, 23, 12, 1, 2, Open)

Don't be afraid to make use of a gentle natural pivot or angle to assist in performing these ripples!

Keep your airstream on, and think of projecting all notes in a steady, straight line, rather than up and down.

A slight inward pull of the upper abdominal muscles can be helpful in producing the top notes of the ripples.

Daily Diagnosstic CHOPCHECKim, cont.

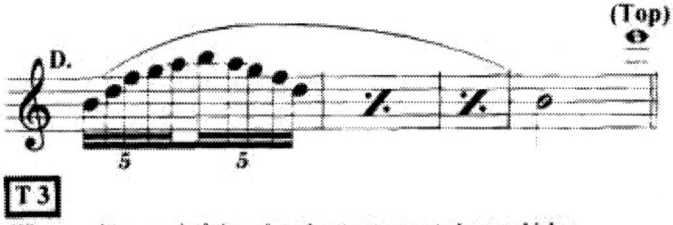

T 3

When you have reached the point where you cannot play any higher, make three attempts (only), then go on to the flow studies.

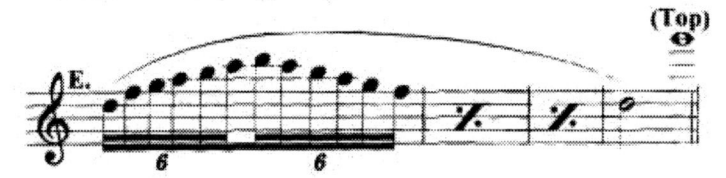

Trying three times keeps you from being frustrated or causing injury to your lips, but sets you up for future success.

These can be repeated through successively higher harmonics as needed.

Follow these ripples with a FLOW study. Examples include Arban's Characteristic Study # 13, or Brandt Orchestral Etude # 31. Focus in flow study is on keeping airstream steady and using as little lip motion as possible.

APPENDIX IV

Equipment Sources & Services

A Sampling of Good Resources for Equipment, Repair, and Information

Bob Reeves
Mouthpieces, including bent shanks, Valve Alignment
http://www.bobreeves.com/

Brad Howland's Website
A great reference site!
www.musicforbrass.com

Charles Colin Music Publishers
A "Best Resource"
www.charlescolin.com
Alan, Liz, Chuck Colin
info@charlescolin.com
212-581-1480

Chop Saver Lip Balm (herbal, all-natural lip salve)
http://www.chopsaver.com/

Clint McLaughlin's Website
http://www.bbtrumpet.com/

Clyde Hunt's Website
http://www.bflatmusic.com/

Dillon Music
East Coast's biggest vendor of trumpets, new or used
http://dillonmusic.com/

Eric Bolvin's Website
(Really Big Songbook, The Arban Manual, etc)
http://www.bolvinmusic.com/

GR Mouthpieces
Computer Designed Trumpet Mouthpieces
www.grmouthpieces.com
Gary Radtke, Brien Scriver
info@grmouthpieces.com
705-715-7060

John Hamaghi, DDS
Website with information about TMJ
http://www.dental--health.com/tmj_depression_treatment.html

Jeff Helgeson's Website
Great resource for Jazz Solo Transcriptions
http://www.shout.net/~jmh/

Longy School
Coursework in Alexander Technique,
Feldenkrais, Dalcroze Eurhythmics
www.longy.edu

Ole J Utnes' Website
One of the most comprehensive resources
on the web for trumpet players
http://abel.hive.no/trumpet/

Osmun Music
The original Boston "Pro Shop"
www.osmun.com
Bob Osmun, Jim Becker
jbecker@osmun.com
Osmun Music
781-646-5756

Rayburn Music
Longstanding Symphony Shop in Boston
www.rayburnmusic.com
617-266-4727

Rich Szabo's Website
(Great source for valve oil, slide grease, breathing advice)
http://www.richszabo.com/

ShulmanSystem
Supportive Device for
Playing the Trumpet
www.ShulmanSystem.com
Matt Shulman
info@shulmansystem.com
718-543-7585

TPIN
Trumpet Players' International Network
Michael Anderson, DMA, moderator
http://www.tpin.org

Trumpet Herald
Website with message boards, classified ads, etc
http://www.trumpetherald.com/

Trumpet Master
Website with message boards, classified ads, etc
http://www.trumpetmaster.com

BIBLIOGRAPHY
Recommended Trumpet Books

(a sampling of excellent references, etudes, etc)
N.B.: It is impossible to list every pertinent book for trumpet,
but this is a good list to start.

Arban, J.B.: *Complete Conservatory Method*

Bateman, D.: *The Complete Trumpet Player* (4 Volumes)
Bolvin, E: *The Arban Manual, Really Big Songbook,
      Lesson Plan & Manuscript Book*
Bousquet: *30 Etudes*

Brahms, J: *12 Etudes for Trumpet*

Brandt, ed. Vacchiano: *Orchestral Studies & Last Etudes*

Broiles, M.: *The Art of Trumpet Playing*
Callet, J.: *Trumpet Yoga, Superchops, Secrets of the Tongue Controlled Embouchure*

Charlier: *36 Etudes Transcendentes*

Clarke, H.: *Characteristic Studies, Technical Studies, Elementary Studies*
Coker, J.: *Patterns for Jazz, Jazz Improvisation*
Colin, Alan: *Beginning Technique, Contemporary Etudes
      Contemporary Atonal Etudes, Close Interval Exercises
      Sequential Studies, Finger Flexibilities*
Colin, Charles: *Lip Flexibility, Volumes 1-2-3; Complete Method*
DiBlasio, Denis: *The Bop Shop, Bop Shop the Sequel*
Durckheim: *Hara, the Vital Center of Man
      The Way of Transformation: Daily Life as Spiritual Practice*
Goode, M.: *Stage Fright in Music and Its Relationship to the Unconscious*
Graves, Matt: *Fundamental Flexibilities*
Green, Barry: *The Inner Game of Music*

Hering, S.: *15 Characteristic Etudes*
Hering, S.: *Trumpet Course*
      (4 Volumes, beginning through advanced intermediate)
      24 Etudes, 32 Etudes, 15 Characteristic Studies

Hickman, D: *Trumpet Pedagogy*
Hunt, C.: *Sailing the Seven C's*
MacDonald, G.: *The Complete Illustrated Guide to the Alexander Technique*
Man-ch'ing, C. & Smith, R.: *T'ai Chi*
Mandino, Og: *The Greatest Salesman in the World*
McLaughlin, C. "Pops": *The Pros Talk Chops, The No-Nonsense Trumpet*

McNeil, John: *Jazz Trumpet Technique*

Merian, L: *Trumpet Isometrics*
Mitchell, H. "Pappy" : Trumpet Course (4 volumes)
Peale, Norman Vincent: *The Power of Positive Thinking*
Provost, Richard: *The Art and Technique of Performance*,
Ristad, E.: *A Soprano on Her Head*
Sanborn, C: *Brass Tactics, Jazz Tactics, Tuning Tactic*
Snitkin, H.: *Practicing for Young Musicians; Practice Planner*
St. Jacome: *Complete Method for Trumpet*
Thompson, Jim & Sayer, Robert: *Buzzing Basics for the Advanced Trumpet Player*
Werner, Kenny: *Effortless Mastery: Liberating the Master Musician Within*
Willey, R: *Bop Duets*, Volumes 1, 2; *Home Cookin' for Young 'Uns (dixieland duets)*
Williams, E.: *Complete Method for Trumpet*

Printed in the United States
98537LV00006B/143/A